TRANSACTIONS
OF THE
AMERICAN PHILOSOPHICAL SOCIETY
Held at Philadelphia for Promoting Useful Knowledge
Vol. 86, Pt. 6

The City-Building Process:
Housing and Services in New Milwaukee Neighborhoods 1880-1910

REVISED EDITION

ROGER D. SIMON

PROFESSOR OF HISTORY, LEHIGH UNIVERSITY

AMERICAN PHILOSOPHICAL SOCIETY
Independence Square • Philadelphia
1996

Library of Congress Catalog Card No.: 78-56724
IBSN:0-87169-685-1
US ISSN 0065 9746

JK

To

Marna, Marci, and Shira

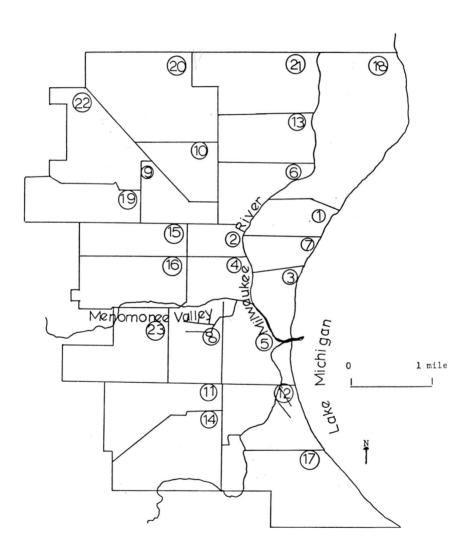

Map 1. Ward map of Milwaukee, 1901-1910.

CONTENTS

THE CITY-BUILDING PROCESS

LIST OF FIGURES, MAPS, AND TABLES

THE CITY-BUILDING PROCESS

MAPS

TABLES

ACKNOWLEDGMENTS

The employees of the city of Milwaukee whom I countered in my research were uniformly interested in the project and eager to cooperate. I am particularly indebted to Mr. Herbert Janusz, Mr. Bert Hartenger, Mr. Walter Powers, and Mr. Louis DeMers for their help in easing my access to various records and providing a place to work. The librarians at the State Historical Society and the Memorial Library of the University of Wisconsin were also most cooperative.

Financial support for various aspects of the research and manuscript preparation came from several sources. The National Science Foundation provided support through Grant GS-921 under the direction of Professor Leo Schnore. I am indebted to Professor Lawrence Leder and Mr. George Jenkins of Lehigh University for helping to secure support from that institution. The University of Wisconsin Graduate School provided grants for travel, keypunching, and computer time.

I am indebted to Mr. Elia Schoomer and Mr. Simon Tickell for assistance in preparing the maps and illustrations. Mrs. Virginia Frey, Mrs. Theresa Racosky, Mrs. Sue Adleman, and the late Mrs. Sallie Ballie typed various portions of the manuscript with care. I know I tested the limits of their patience.

A portion of chapter 4 appeared as an article under the title "Housing and Services in an Immigrant Neighborhood: Milwaukee's Ward 14,'" in the *Journal of Urban History* 2: pp. 435-458. I am indebted to Professor Raymond Mohl, who was then the editor, for his comments and to Sage Publications, Inc. for permission to reprint material from the article.

My wife and daughter provided much needed moral support and enthusiasm in the late stages of the project.

This study has benefited greatly from the comments and suggestions of a number of scholars. I am indebted to them and they deserve a share of the credit for whatever merits this study may possess; they are absolved of blame in its defects. Professor John Ottensmann of the University of California, Irvine, shared his analysis of Milwaukee census tract data with me and provided several helpful suggestions. University of Wisconsin Professors Morton Rothstein, Stanley K. Schultz, Leo F. Schnore and David Ward and Professor William Shade of Lehigh all provided valuable suggestions and comments. Professor Sam Bass Warner, Jr. of Boston University read both the original proposal and the dissertation.

Professor Eric E. Lampard, now of the State University of New

York, Stony Brook, guided this project from its inception and read the manuscript at several stages. The entire project has benefitted greatly from his careful analysis and his insights.

R.D.S.

———••••••———

In preparing the revised edition a number of people have been particularly helpful. I am indebted to Professor Margo Anderson at the University of Wisconsin--Milwaukee for her continuing interest in this work and for facilitating a research trip to Milwaukee. Stanley Mallach, John Gurda, and Paul Jakubovitz were all very generous with their time, and shared their insights on changes in the city. Anthony Orum generously shared with me an advance copy of his new book, *City-Building in America*.

At Lehigh University John Gatewood helped to solve some statistical problems, and Roseann Bowerman was exceptionally helpful in obtaining census publications. The Office of Research provided financial support. Carole LeFaivre-Rochester at the American Philosophical Society suggested the revised edition and guided the manuscript through the publication process with skill and patience. And most important of all, my wife, Marna, has been unwavering in her support throughout my career.

A NOTE ON THE TEXT

Many Milwaukee street names and almost all street numbers have changed since the turn of the century. For ease of identification, 1977 street names and numbers have been used throughout. The only exceptions are ward maps which date from the 1890's. For a complete cross-reference of old and new street numbers see *Wright's Street Guide Supplement to Wright's City Directory 1930, 1931.*

Throughout the citations, Milwaukee and Wisconsin are abbreviated as Milw. and Wis.

I. INTRODUCTION: URBAN HISTORY AND THE CITY-BUILDING PROCESS

NOTHING LASTS forever, especially in America, but houses are among our most enduring structures—indeed they outlast such monumental structures as skyscrapers and baseball stadiums. A large fraction of the homes built in American cities around the turn of the century are still occupied. The characteristics of the homes and neighborhoods created at that time affected the quality of life for both initial and subsequent residents. These attributes included the size of the house lots, the dimensions and pattern of the streets, the size and amenity level of the homes, the number of dwelling units in the structure, and whether factories were scattered through residential streets. As a leading urban historian noted, "differential environments might be accommodative or dysfunctional. Without subscribing to an environmental determinism, one can acknowledge that environment performs enabling and constraining functions. It provides or inhibits satisfactions throughout the life cycle...."[1] Thus, attributes of housing affected personal and family privacy, and standards of cleanliness and good health. How parks, play spaces, schools, and churches were sited could facilitate or discourage a sense of community.

The mechanism by which open or vacant land at the city's edge was turned into an urban environment is what we mean by the city-building process. This study will examine three peripheral districts of Milwaukee, Wisconsin, and trace their evolution from open farm land to city neighborhoods. We will also revisit those neighborhoods during the twentieth century to assess how they fared and how they served, or failed to serve, their residents over time.

Milwaukee was selected because in many ways it was representative of a particular group of Great Lakes industrial cities that experienced explosive population growth in the last third of the nineteenth century as they became the locus of much of the country's heavy industry. They attracted large numbers of the European immigrants pouring into the country in the last decades of the century. They grew so quickly that they had to scramble to provide housing for their new residents. Since it is always difficult to assess how a single case study exemplifies the larger pattern, we will place Milwaukee in the context of these other

---

1 Lubove, 1967: p. 34; see also comments by Warner, 1972: p. 199; Schnore, 1963: ch. 1 and pp. 141-142; Glazer, 1967: pp. 140-163.

cities as we proceed.

At the time this study was conceived in 1968, only one historian, Sam Bass Warner, Jr., had examined the process of development of peripheral urban land. Warner's study, *Streetcar Suburbs,* analyzed the development of three residential areas of Boston from 1870 to 1900.[2] In the past two decades there have been several other in-depth analyses of the city-building process in various cities covering the same era. The most notable of these are Oliver Zunz's *The Changing Face of Inequality* on Detroit, Ann Durkin Keating's *Building Chicago,* and Michael Doucet and John Weaver's *Housing the North American City* on Hamilton, Ontario. A number of other studies have dealt with aspects of city-building or its implications.[3]

The literature of the city-building process, including this study, has fleshed out the distinct, albeit overlapping, steps in the creation of the built environment. The distinct steps are subdivision, improvement in accessibility, financing and construction of homes, provision of infrastructure services (water, sewers, paved streets, electricity, and gas), peopling the neighborhood, and opportunities for homeownership.[4]

Subdivision refers to the division of a farm or parcel of vacant land into house lots for resale to builders or other investors. The subdivider's goal was usually speculative with the expectation that the lots would be resold to other investors or directly to builders, either prospective residents or contractors. They were sensitive to the social class and financial resources of buyers likely to purchase lots in their tract. Subdividers anticipated purchase by families living in the adjacent built-up portion of the city. In almost all cases subdividers cut up their tracts into long narrow blocks and divided those blocks into long narrow lots, each with some street frontage, but with as few streets as possible. There was no profit in streets.[5]

Subdivision and lot sales did not proceed in a steady and even

---

2 Warner, 1962; for essays calling for attention to the urban physical environment, see Lampard, 1961: pp. 49-61; Lampard, 1963, pp. 225-247; Lubove, 1967: pp. 33-39; Warner, 1968a: pp. 26-43.

3 Zunz, 1982; Keating, 1988; Doucet and Weaver, 1991; see also Marsh, 1990; Ebner, 1988; Edel, Sclar, and Luria, 1984, von Hoffman, 1994; on the twentieth-century developers, see Weiss, 1987. For reviews of the literature, see Doucet, 1982; Muller, 1987; Tarr and Konvitz, 1987; Gillette, 1990.

4 Doucet and Weaver, 1991: pp. 21, 23, presents a schematic of a residential development model.

5 Warner, 1962: pp. 61, 121, 132-141; Reps, 1965: p. 302; Doucet and Weaver, 1991: chs. 1-2; Keating, 1988: pp. 64-68.

pattern, either spatially or over time. Temporal distortions occurred because those operations were sensitive to the cyclical fluctuations of the economy. Homer Hoyt, an economist and real estate analyst, studied Chicago land values over a hundred-year period and identified a "real estate cycle" which corresponded closely with the business cycles. Hoyt, Warner, and others found that the land subdivided in one cycle often lay undeveloped until the next. Subdividers could be caught by shifting trends during those intervening decades, which might require redividing a parcel into smaller lots, or causing a loss on the investment.[6]

The nineteenth century witnessed a succession of public transit innovations: omnibus, steam railway, horsecar, cable car, and electric streetcar. Each technology, by extending the range and speed of common carriers while keeping fares low, enlarged the area for home-sites. Subdivision usually preceded the arrival of streetcar service. The subdivider, anticipating greater access to his land, sought to get in early and enjoy the considerable capital gain that would follow from greater accessibility.[7] In much of the late nineteenth century subdivision was a small-scale form of speculation, although in some places streetcar companies or their principal owners were active subdividers. In many cases the streetcar company made more money on subdivision than on providing service. There were also instances of real estate associations engaged in larger scale development. These enterprises focused on development for middle- and upper-income families which required larger capital investment and might take longer to realize a return.[8]

In some instances the subdivider sought to develop a more comprehensive urban environment than simply platted lots and graded, unpaved streets. Such a commitment meant a community for middle- and upperincome residents and entailed making additional investment in the parcel. Under those circumstances a subdivider needed to select a section of town away from factories, near topographic amenities, and having or likely to acquire some prestige value. Generous landscaping was essential. The most important step was to lay out larger than

6 Hoyt, 1933: pp. 369, 372, Appendix I; Blank, 1954: pp. 41-42; Fellman, 1957: pp. 62, 67-70, 77; Monchow, 1939: pp. 3-36, 56-57, 75-76; Doucet and Weaver, 1991: pp. 27-54, 87-102. See the episode of Lester Kane's failed subdivision speculation in *Jennie Gerhardt*, Dreiser, 1989: pp. 326-334.

7 Warner, 1962: pp. 21-29; Zunz, 1984: p. 125; Edel, Sclar, and Luria, 1984: ch. 2.; Keating, 1988: pp. 22-26, 65-68.

8 Doucet and Weaver, 1991: pp. 87-102; Keating, 1988: pp. 66-68; Zunz, 1984: 161-176; Jackson, 1985: pp. 116-124.

average lots and more generous streets.[9] Restrictive covenants in deeds could help assure buyers that their investment would be protected. These restrictions usually required a house of a minimum size, and sometimes of a minimum cost, and a standard set-back from the street. Covenants prohibited adverse uses such as factories, stables, or taverns. Thus the subdivider with patience and assets could truly shape a community. Before the 1910s this was possible only for the most exclusive communities.[10] After the parcel was fully developed the importance of the restrictions declined. The restrictions on building had the effect of neighborhood zoning, and since the subdivider and initial tenants had a mutual interest in maintaining land values, the covenants were effective in creating neighborhoods homogeneous as to both residences and residents.[11]

Another critical dimension in shaping the character of a new subdivision and attracting buyers was the provision of the infrastructure, notably water mains, sewers, sidewalks, and paved streets. Aggressive subdividers might install sidewalks or sewers on empty blocks on the expectation that the resultant appreciation in land values would repay the initial expense. But such blocks sometimes remained partially or wholly empty for years.[12] As a block began to fill with homes some cities paid for those improvements out of general tax revenue, while in other communities special assessments taxed the owners for at least part of the cost. In such cases politicians were usually sensitive to the owners' wishes. Special assessments also meant affluent owners could accelerate installations while those with a more limited income could delay the services, trading inconvenience and higher morbidity and mortality for lower immediate tax bills. In the 1880s and 1890s early residents might have to wait a few years for water mains and sewer lines. After the turn of the century middle- and upper-middle class home buyers expected those services to be in place. This study examines in detail the relationship between provision of services and the extent of development of

9 On subdivision in fashionable neighborhoods and exclusive suburbs, see Jackson, 1985: chs. 4-5; Ebner, 1988: ch. 1; Marsh, 1990: ch. 4; O'Connor, 1983, pp. 5-10; Wright, 1981: pp. 95-96.

10 Jackson, 1985: chs. 3-4; Stillgoe, 1988: part III; Marsh, 1990: chs. 3-4.

11 Doucet and Weaver, 1991: pp. 99-102; Keating, 1988: ch. 4; O'Connor, pp. 5-6; Stach, 1988.

12 Hoyt, 1933: pp. 90-91, 180, 392. See, for example, the illustrations in Mayer and Wade, 1969: pp. 166-167.

particular blocks for neighborhoods of different socioeconomic groups.[13]

In jurisdictions outside the city limits subdividers often used annexation as a device to gain access to city services and hence make their properties more attractive to middle class customers. Cities also used services as an inducement to encourage outlying areas to accept annexation.[14]

The style and size of new homes built at the edges of large cities varied depending upon the city's size and density, rate of growth, and local custom. In upper Manhattan, Brooklyn, Philadelphia, Baltimore, and Washington the row house prevailed. In New York the "brownstones" were quite large and often included rental units at the outset. Elsewhere they were smaller and intended for one family. The row house provided a small private yard in back, and because each home was on its own lot, maximized the opportunity for homeownership. In Boston and other New England cities two- or three-story units, or flats, were common. These large double- and triple-deckers may actually have provided more square footage than small row homes, but they were built very close together and cut out much of the sunlight and fresh air which were one of the periphery's attractions. They also limited homeowning opportunities.[15]

In the middle west single family wood frame houses were the standard. As housing and land costs rose, the double-decker became more prevalent. Here too local custom led to some deviations. Milwaukee had a higher percentage of double-deckers than Detroit and Cleveland, but in all cities modest setbacks and backyards on 3,600-4,000 square foot lots provided more open space and lower density than in the row house cities or Boston's Roxbury and Dorchester sections.[16]

Building of new homes on peripheral sites was largely a decentralized, small-scale enterprise. Financing was so problematic that large developments were rarely possible although there were a few large scale contractors. In the working class neighborhoods there is considerable evidence that buyers constructed small cottages themselves or with the help of neighbors, with the expectation of adding on to them later.[17]

---

13 Warner, 1962: pp. 61, 31, 138; Doucet and Weaver, 1991: pp. 95-96, 107; Zunz, 1982: pp. 113-128, 169; Keating, 1988: pp. 71-78.

14 Keating, 1988: ch. 6; Fleischmann, 1988; Warner, 1962: pp. 163-164.

15 Warner: 1962: pp. 52-66, chs. 5 and 7; on row houses of Philadelphia, see Sutherland, 1973: pp. 173-201.

16 Zunz, 1982: pp. 156-157.

17 Zunz, 1982: pp. 152-176; Doucet and Weaver, 1991: ch. 2.

The size and amenity level of new homes largely followed from the subdividers' earlier expectations and level of investment: small lots without water and sewer lines kept costs as low as possible for working class buyers, while the middle and upper middle class buyers were attracted to larger lots and with infrastructure in place. Despite the relative decentralization of the entire process, a remarkable degree of homogeneity emerged at the level of individual neighborhoods, as Warner pointed out in *Streetcar Suburbs*.[18]

Students of American cities have offered a variety of explanations as to why families moved to the urban periphery. Lloyd Rodwin, an urban planner, characterized the urban expansion of the late nineteenth century as a search for a "functionally adequate physical environment." Noting that the characteristics of such an environment vary in time and place, he suggested as some of the more desirable traits of such an environment: "adequate access to employment centers for the principal and secondary wage earner... physical settings providing adequate and attractive housing, open space, traffic safety, and recreation areas."[19] Such an environment, in particular, met the needs of families with growing children. Both historians and contemporary social scientists emphasize the attractiveness of a low-density or suburban environment for raising children, and identify that sector of the city with the child-raising years of the life cycle.

Warner argued that a suburbanizing move was a reaction to the inner city congestion, a yearning for a "rural ideal" that glorified the countryside for its simplicity, natural beauty, harmony, and sense of community. "The rural ideal, by its emphasis on the pleasures of private family life, on the security of a small community setting, and on the enjoyment of natural surroundings, encouraged the middle class to build a wholly new residential environment: the modern suburb."[20] Warner's argument has been amply seconded by subsequent studies, and it is not necessary to separate the search for modern and spacious homes from the cultural and emotional satisfactions for a putative rural ideal.[21]

In *Streetcar Suburbs* Warner suggested that a move to a peripheral

---

18 Warner, 1962: ch. 6; Zunz, 1982: p. 7; Doucet and Weaver, 1991: pp. 74-75 found less homogeneity in pre-1880 neighborhoods.

19 Rodwin, 1959: p. 118; see also Vance, 1967: pp. 126-127; Chudacoff, 1972: pp. 153, 158-159.

20 Warner, 1962: p. 14.

21 The most extensive treatment of the concept is by Stillgoe, 1988; see also Stillgoe, 1983: ch. 10; Jackson, 1985: chs. 3 and 4; Marsh, 1990; Ebner, 1988: ch. 3.

neighborhood was open to roughly the upper income half of the population. He argued that the effect of the interaction among subdivision, streetcar extension, and the aspirations of the would-be residents was to segregate socioeconomic groups by income level but not by ethnicity. Thus at any given time, the wealthiest were to be found along a band of land at the periphery of the metropolis while the lower middle class occupied the zone nearest to the older city. The workers in the lower middle class lacked the job permanence of the central and upper middle class, and often had more than one wage earner in the home. Thus, they needed the flexibility that crosstown streetcar service provided, and such service was only available in the more densely settled portions of the periphery.[22] Consequently, their more limited resources and need for group transportation led to overcrowding the landscape and belied any true rural or suburban landscape. The correlation between distance and socioeconomic class composition was only weakened where unique features of topography or delayed provision of crosstown service distorted its impact on the distribution of the urban population. Thus, Warner viewed the process of urban expansion as one in which the occupational requirements and income levels of different groups tied them to various levels of transit service.[23]

By looking at a smaller city, we can see that there were neighborhoods constructed for various socioeconomic groups, and that such groups overlapped heavily with ethnicity. As this and subsequent studies show, there were new peripheral neighborhoods built for almost all segments of the population.[24] Working class ethnic neighborhoods provided a basis for the creation of ethnically-based entrepreneurs and social institutions—religious, recreational, mutually beneficial—which, in turn, nurtured indigenous leadership. These communities provided a valuable transition for first- and second-generation immigrant groups into broader American culture.[25]Middle-class families sought to separate themselves from the lower status newer immigrant and working-class neighborhoods. They wished their children to learn and to play with

---

22 Warner, 1962: pp. 52-66 and ch. 5.

23 Warner, 1962: pp. 21-22, 32, 46, 58, 60, 64-66, 86-92; Ward, 1971: pp. 128-143, developed Warner's findings into a broader model; von Hoffman, 1994, modified Warner's findings considerably for the Jamaica Plain neighborhood of Boston, demonstrating a considerable mixture of ethnic and occupational groups and a sense of community identification.

24 See also Zunz, 1982: chs. 2, 3, 6.

25 Bodnar, Simon, and Weber, 1982: pp. 79-82, 161, 200-202; Zunz, ch. 7; Cohen, 1990: ch. 2; Rosenzweig, 1985.

others of a similar social background.[26]

At the turn of the century only a minority of residents in peripheral neighborhoods were homeowners. Income, ethnicity, and age of the family head were all factors in explaining homeownership patterns. Homeowning was not restricted to the more affluent socioeconomic groups. Not only did immigrants and laborers move into new housing at the periphery but in many cases they were able to purchase their homes.[27] Down payments were high, often 40 or 50 percent, with the mortgages due in five to twelve years; buyers expected to refinance several times before retiring their debt.[28] For working class families to raise $1,000 and pay off a debt of another $1,500 required enormous sacrifice. Stephan Thernstrom, noting homeownership as a principal form of property mobility among Irish immigrants, described the sacrifices endured by homeowning families as "ruthless underconsumption." Certainly they lived in overcrowded conditions, with homes built for one family occupied by two.[29] This study will examine in detail how these priorities manifest themselves in Milwaukee and the trade-off working class families made in order to own.

The merits of homeownership for working class families have been the subject of some heated debate. Notably, Edel, Sclar, and Luria have argued that it retarded social and geographic mobility and was a poor investment for working class families. Others have pointed out that not only did immigrants explicitly want to be homeowners, perhaps as a concrete manifestation of economic independence, but that the alternatives to ownership may not have been other forms of investment, but expenditure on other goods. Michael Doucet and John Weaver provide the most comprehensive critique of the Edel, Sclar and Luria argument.[30] This study examines in detail the characteristics of homeowning families.[31]

This study does not address equally all of the stages in the process.

---

26 Wright, 1981: 175.

27 Warner, 1962: p. 120; Rodwin, 1959: pp. 34-39; Bodnar, Simon, and Weber, 1982: ch. 6; Thernstrom, 1964: ch. 5. and pp. 152-165, 199-200. For a contemporary observation see Byington, 1910: pp. 56-62, 131-132, 152-155.

28 Warner, 1962: pp. 117-120; Bodnar, Simon, and Weber, 1982: ch. 6; Zunz, 1982: pp. 161-162; Doucet and Weaver, 1991: ch. 6.

29 Thernstrom, 1964: ch. 5, quote p. 136; see also Zunz, 1982: pp. 172, 174.

30 Edel, Sclar and Luria, 1984; Doucet and Weaver, 1991: ch. 4.

31 See also Zunz, 1982: pp. 152-176; Bodnar, Simon, and Weber, 1982: ch. 6; Doucet and Weaver, 1991: ch. 7.

It was conceived and originally researched less than a decade after *Streetcar Suburbs* and was stimulated by the findings and insights of that study, but also took as a given certain aspects of the process that later historians have revised, particularly the role of subdividers and builders. The focus here is on the class and ethnic diversity of the new neighborhoods, the new residents' ability to use special assessments for improvements to exercise some control over their environment, and their remarkable ability to become homeowners.

RESEARCH DESIGN AND SOURCES

The examination of the city-building process requires a detailed inspection of particular blocks and lots. One must determine the timing of subdivision, street layout and paving, water and sewer mains, streetcar lines, schools, and dwellings. The timing of these developments, in turn, can be associated with certain indicators of amenity and convenience: lot and street size, distance from the central business district and other employment centers, proximity to parks, rivers, or lakes, size and type of the housing stock. It is possible to study the city-building process at that level only by sampling a portion of the expanding periphery. Several approaches were possible: focusing on one wedge or sector of the metropolitan area, focusing on a continuous zone of three to four miles from the city center, or selecting a number of peripheral wards in different directions. The latter design is followed here for several important reasons.

Basing an analysis of urban development on city wards entails certain risks; a ward is an artificial and arbitrary unit of space. It is not necessarily a neighborhood, homogeneous in either demographic or physical characteristics. Natural or man-made barriers may sometimes divide it into distinct sections; or, in the absence of any topographic features, it *may* merge with the rest of the city surrounding it, altogether lacking distinguishing or unifying characteristics. A sufficient reason for undertaking a study of urban expansion by examining individual wards is the availability of certain kinds of data only at the ward level. We can make statements about selected peripheral wards which we probably cannot make, for example, about a continuous zone of land around the entire fringe of the city.

It was neither feasible nor necessary to study the evolution of peripheral wards by examining the development of every block and every street. By the use of random sampling techniques, it was possible to reduce the area actually studied to manageable proportions without invalidating the analysis or distorting its findings. Consequently, the data presented are based on a 10 percent random sample drawn from the facing street blocks of four peripheral wards. The sample was stratified to provide proportions of horizontal, vertical, and diagonal blocks equal to that appearing in each ward. Facing street blocks rather than square blocks were used because the city installed its services down the middle of the street and serviced the houses on both sides. Within the sample blocks all possible data were gathered; that is, the data for any given block are not a sample.

The sample is thus one of space, not of houses or inhabitants. To have taken a sample of houses or families would have changed the focus of the study. The primary interest here is the timing and means by which peripheral space was taken over by an expanding city. A sample of houses would skip over undeveloped space and blocks with lots that remained vacant after the date selected for the sample year.

The present research design precludes an analysis of the activity of individual builders and developers. To have studied this group directly would have involved ascertaining all the homes built by certain men regardless of location. This might be valuable, but would have resulted in a somewhat different kind of study.[32]

The main sources of data for the analysis were the original building permits, the city tax rolls, the city directories, and the 1905 Wisconsin state census rolls. Each source had its limitations, and it was only by using all available systematic sources that a reasonably complete set of data could be generated. The building permits provided the date of construction, intended use, dimensions, number of floors, type of materials used, and estimated cost. Dwelling costs, as reported on the building permits, are presented for some dwellings merely as suggestive of a given price range rather than indicative of the actual construction cost or sale price.

Milwaukee first required building permits in 1888, although compliance was not total.[33] The tax rolls were checked again in 1905 to locate buildings constructed between 1888 and 1905 for which no permit was ever filed, or for which the permit was subsequently lost. In the tables below there are separate entries for buildings built before 1888 and

---

32 Warner, 1962: pp. 126-132, 184-185 for discussion and data on the small-scale home builders typical of the period.

33 Milw., 1888: ch. III. The building permits are filed by address in the Office of the Building Inspector, Milw.

for buildings built sometime between 1888 and 1905.[34] The Sanborn Map Company published fire insurance atlases for Milwaukee in 1894 and 1910 which showed every dwelling in the city and indicated the number of floors, use, and type of building material. Those atlases supplemented the permits and tax rolls.[35]

The Wisconsin state census rolls for 1905 provided the demographic and social data. The manuscripts recorded the complete name of every family member, his or her age, relation to the head of house, birthplace, parents' birthplace, and occupation. The census also included questions on the number of months employed and tenancy status (rented or owned, with or without a mortgage). The census rolls suffered from the defects of all census canvasses. Undoubtedly, the complete population was not interviewed, and the poor were more likely to avoid, or be avoided by, the census taker. When no one was present at a home, the enumerator often sought information from a neighbor or just failed to return. Nevertheless, the census did make the effort at a city-wide canvass, and we can supplement its information with the tax rolls and city directories.[36] (See Appendix A for a further discussion on the use of the 1905 Wisconsin census rolls.)

The only adjustment made to the data was in aggregating the occupations into socioeconomic categories. Several historians have pointed out that different occupational classifications serve different purposes.[37] Studies of occupational structure, of status, and of social mobility all call for different occupational classifications. The socioeconomic categories are used here to suggest ability to pay for housing. There are nine occupational categories in this study: (1) professionals; (2) major proprietors, managers, and officials; (3) semi-professionals; (4) white collar clerical workers; (5) shopkeepers and other petty propri-

---

34 For some blocks it was not possible to use the tax rolls effectively because the blocks were not formally subdivided; if houses on such blocks did not have a permit they are listed as being built "sometime before 1905." Milw., Tax office, MS. Tax Rolls.

35 Sanborn and Perris Map Co., 1894; Sanborn Map Co., 1910. These maps were updated annually on a subscription basis. The State Hist. Soc. of Wis. has both an original and an updated set of the 1894 ed. and an updated set of the 1910 ed. The Library of Congress, Map Division has original sets of both editions. See also Baist, 1898. See Simon, 1971: Appendix C for a complete list of the sample blocks with both old and new street names.

36 Wis. Sec. of State, 1905. If census data were available for a family but the occupation was blank, the occupation listed in *Wright's City Directory* was used. For further discussion on the validity of the census as a data source see Warner, 1962: Appendix A. On city directories see Knights, 1971: Appendix A.

37 Katz, 1972: pp. 63-88; Thernstrom, 1973: pp. 47-48.

etors, minor officials; (6) skilled workers; 7) semi-skilled workers; (8) unskilled workers; (9) unknown, retired, widowed, unemployed. These classifications are the same as those used by Peter Knights in his study of antebellum Boston's population and Kathleen Conzen in *Immigrant Milwaukee*. They are parallel to those used, among others, by Stephan Thernstrom in *The Other Bostonians*.[38]

Certainly there was considerable variation in family income within the categories listed. Not only might two carpenters have widely varying family incomes, but one who was exceptionally able might earn more than a policeman, bookkeeper, or small proprietor. The worker's age, native ability, industriousness, ethnic background, luck, and the number of other working people in his family would all influence family income. His wealth would depend, in addition to his income , on his age, family size, luck, and frugality. But we do have measures of age, family size, and ethnicity to supplement our data, and evidence from the time period suggests a very high correlation between occupation and income.[39]

The study is divided into two parts. The first half will focus on the city-wide changes in Milwaukee during the period 1880-1910. It will consider the geography and economy and how the interaction of those basic factors shaped the land use patterns of the city. It will examine the housing stock and the city's policy towards such services as pure water, sewers, and streets. Finally it will measure the residential segregation of the population by occupation, ethnicity, and families with children. The second part of the study will examine the process of shaping a physical environment in three distinctive peripheral neighborhoods during the same time period. Attention will focus primarily on the creation of a peripheral housing stock and the establishment of those services essential to a healthy and functionally adequate environment. The relationship of this new environment to its population is examined in close detail in order to understand for whom the new environment was created and what kinds of people selected and, presumably, preferred a peripheral location.

---

38 See Simon, 1971: Appendix D for a complete list of the occupations in each category. See also Knights, 1971 : Appendix E; Thernstrom, 1973: Appendix B; Conzen, 1976: Appendix.

39 Wis. Bureau of Labor, Census, and Industrial Statistics, 1896: part V.

2. MILWAUKEE: THE CONTEXT FOR GROWTH

For the growth of a city is a cumulative as well as a cyclical process. Each successive building, railroad line, streetcar line, or park leaves a permanent impress upon the character of the city. A pattern begins to form at the very outset that with the lapse of time acquires a certain rigidity. The railroad or park system once laid down holds its position through great changes.[1]

TO UNDERSTAND the city-building process, we must first examine the city as a whole. As Homer Hoyt aptly pointed out, the decisions made at the outset, the grid-pattern, the transit system, and the developing housing stock at any given time, limit the possibility for what one subdivider, builder, or would-be owner can do to change or influence the environment. An examination of the city as a whole is also necessary to understand how the peculiarities of demography, geography, economy, housing, and services in Milwaukee affected the kinds of new neighborhoods built there at the turn of the century.

EARLY GROWTH

The mouth of the Milwaukee River offers the best naturally protected harbor on the west side of Lake Michigan between Chicago and Green Bay. The Milwaukee River is not a major avenue to the interior, but it does join two smaller streams, the Menomonee River and Kinnickinnic Creek, just before its mouth. The Milwaukee and Menomonee rivers cut the area into three distinct sections. The Milwaukee, coming down from the north near the lake, marks off a narrow peninsula to its east. This east-side peninsula features imposing bluffs overlooking the lake about two miles north of the river's mouth. The Menomonee flows from the west and cuts a valley about three-quarters of a mile wide for a distance of three miles. Consequently, the Menomonee Valley was a barrier sufficient to create two more distinct sections.

In the exuberant land speculations of the 1830's each section found its own promoter, thus three separate and competing settlements arose around the mouth of the Milwaukee.[2] Even after the three settlements

---

1 Hoyt, 1933: p. 6.

2 Whitbeck, 1921: pp. 41, 45; see *Built In Milwaukee*, 1983, for an outstanding pictorial history of the city's development.

merged, they maintained considerable autonomy as separate wards of the new Town of Milwaukee.[3] Separate improvement funds for each ward continued as a permanent feature of Milwaukee's development[4].

Townsite speculation also influenced the original plat. The promoters followed the checkerboard gridiron plan used in designing most nineteenth-century western towns. The gridiron was the easiest plat to survey and provided a large number of uniform lots which were simply described in legal documents. It also appeared to be a rational plan, which the nonresident speculator or visitor could grasp without difficulty.[5]

The importance of the original plats also lay in their continuous extension. In 1856 the state legislature stipulated that any person or group of persons desiring to subdivide any property in Milwaukee into city lots "shall, in platting the same, cause the streets and alleys in such plat to correspond in width and general direction with the streets and alleys in said city adjacent to . . ." their holdings[6]. Thus, one of the most critical decisions affecting the physical appearance of the city and its ability to function as a place for the exchange of goods, labor and information occurred at the very earliest stage of the city's development. The private interests of the speculator and the promoter largely determined the design and form of Milwaukee .[7]

Nonetheless, the promotion of Milwaukee was spectacularly successful. In the 1840's alone the site grew from a village of 1,712 to a small city of 20,061, a 1,071 percent increase. By the end of the Civil War it was a major city of over 50,000, and it surpassed 100,000 a decade later. By the end of the century its population was over a quarter million, and it grew by almost a total of 100,000 in the next decade. Meanwhile, by a sequence of annexations, the city's area grew from less than twelve square miles in 1846 to almost twenty-four square miles in 1910, with most of the increment taking place after 1880.

In 1910 Milwaukee had 373,857 residents, ranking twelfth largest,

---

3 Still, 1948: ch. 1; Conzen, 1976: ch. 1.

4 Still, 1948: pp. 33-37; Larson, 1908: pp. 12, 14.

5 Vliet, 1835; Reps, 1965: pp. 294-299, 302.

6 Milw., 1861: pp. 94-98; Wis., 1874: ch. VI, sec. 25 (sec. 31 after 1887).

7 The theme of privatism receives extensive treatment in Warner, 1968; see also Warner, 1972: ch. 2. On the significance of the gridiron in Milw., see Hegemann, 1916: pp. 9-10, 22. Compare with Nolen, 1915: pp. 33-53; Nolen, 1929: pp. 31-42, 90; Hoyt, 1933: pp. 288, 426-433; Warner, 1962; pp. 132-141.

and a metropolitan area population of 427,175, ranking fifteenth largest. Her city population was just slightly larger than that of Cincinnati, and her metropolitan area population almost the same as that of Los Angeles. Table 1 shows the population growth of the city from 1840 to 1910, and table 2 compares the population and rankings of all cities over 200,000 in 1910.

THE ECONOMY AND INDUSTRIAL LOCATION

The basis of Milwaukee's early growth lay in the vital commercial and processing functions it performed for a fertile and growing hinterland. Aided by an expanding railroad network and harbor improvements, the city became in the 1860's and 1870's a leading center of flour milling, slaughtering and packing, tanning, and brewing. Her growth in the late nineteenth century, however, lay primarily in the development of heavy industry. At Milwaukee and other Great Lakes ports, industrialists could bring together, at low cost, the main ingredients for iron

TABLE 1

POPULATION GROWTH OF MILWAUKEE, 1840–1910

Year	Population	Percentage Increase Over Previous Decade
1840	1,712	
1850	20,061	1,071.8
1860	45,246	125.5
1870	71,440	57.9
1880	115,587	61.8
1890	204,468	76.9
1900	285,315	39.5
1910	373,857	31.0

Sources: U.S. Dept. of State, 1843: p. 461; 1853: p. 922; U.S. Dept. of Interior, 1864: p. 539; U.S. Bureau of the Census, 1883: p. 370; 1912: 1: p. 670.

TABLE 2

POPULATION, VALUE ADDED IN MANUFACTURING, AND SHARE OF LABOR FORCE IN ALL MANUFACTURING OF LARGEST U.S. CITIES, 1910

Cities Ranked by Population, 1910[a]	Population 1910	Value added by Manufacture, 1909 ($ millions)	Rank[b]	Per cent male work force in all Manufacturing[c] 1910	Rank[d]
1. New York (NYC)	4,766.9	937.5	1	42.3	16
2. Chicago (Chi.)	2,185.3	487.7	2	46.1	12
3. Philadelphia (Phil.)	1,549.0	317.0	3	50.3	8*
4. St. Louis (St.L.)	687.0	140.3	4	44.6	13
5. Boston (Bstn.)	670.6	112.9	7	39.1	19
6. Cleveland (Clvl.)	560.7	117.0	6	56.5	3
7. Baltimore (Balt.)	558.5	80.0	13	43.6	15
8. Pittsburgh (Pitt.)	533.9	94.9	8	51.3	7
9. Detroit (Detr.)	465.8	122.8	5	58.6	1
10. Buffalo (Buff.)	423.7	82.3	12	50.3	8*
11. San Francisco (S.F.)	416.9	56.8	15	33.8	27
12. Milwaukee (Milw.)	373.9	87.7	11	56.9	2
13. Cincinnati (Cinc.)	363.6	92.6	9	47.7	11
14. Newark (Nwrk.)	347.5	87.8	10	56.0	4
15. New Orleans (N.O.)	339.1	30.1	28	34.6	24

Continuation of Table 2.

16. Washington (Wash.)	331.1	15.0		30.2	28
17. Los Angeles (L.A.)	319.2	29.7	29	34.5	25*
18. Minneapolis (Mpls.)	301.4	45.4	18	41.6	17
19. Jersey City (Jr. C.)	267.8	39.5	21	38.7	20
20. Kansas City, Mo. (K.C.)	248.4	23.7	39	34.5	25*
21. Seattle (Sttl.)	237.2	21.9	44	35.6	22*
22. Indianapolis (Inpl.)	233.7	42.4	20	48.9	10
23. Providence (Prov.)	224.3	55.5	16	55.4	5
24. Louisville (Loui.)	223.9	47.1	17	44.3	14
25. Rochester (Roch.)	218.1	62.0	14	55.0	6
26. St. Paul (St.P.)	214.7	28.7	30	36.9	21
27. Denver (Denv.)	213.4	20.6	51	35.6	22*
28. Portland, Ore. (Port.)	207.2	20.8	49	40.1	18

[a] The accompanying abbreviations are used for these cities in subsequent tables in the text.
[b] Ranking based on all cities with largest value of product.
[c] Percentage of all males over ten years of age in all mechanical and manufacturing occupations as classified by the census.
[d] Ranking based only on cities listed in table.
* Tied for the same rank.
Sources: U.S. Bureau of the Census, 1912: 1: pp. 73–75; 1912a: 8: p. 84; 1912b: 4: pp. 152–207.

and later, steel production: Pennsylvania and Illinois coal, with Michigan, Wisconsin, and Minnesota ores. By 1909 the foundries, machine shops, iron and steel mills, and tool and implements firms together constituted the largest single manufacturing industry in the city.[8]

Although Milwaukee rose from a commercial base, its work force was, by 1910, more heavily committed to manufacturing of all types than most other cities of its size. Although Milwaukee was then the country's twelfth largest city, it ranked eleventh in value added by manufacture, tenth in value of manufactured products, seventh in value added per capita, and second in the percentage of its male work force engaged in all manufacturing and mechanical pursuits. It stood with Buffalo, Cleveland, and Detroit, all Great Lakes ports, in the high proportion of manufacturing workers in its labor force. This large industrial work force, which overlapped the foreign-born component of the population, affected the city-building process by imposing particular needs and constraints on the location and type of new housing. Table 2 compares Milwaukee's commitment to heavy industry with other large cities.

A labor force heavily weighted towards manufacturing where relatively low wages, long hours, and irregular work prevailed, meant that the location of work would exert an exceptionally strong force on residential location. Industrialists strove to locate where they could effect the greatest economies, and usually left the workers to secure whatever housing they could. Topography, geography, transportation facilities and the early town rivalries all influenced the location of Milwaukee's industrial and commercial land uses. Specialized uses appeared early in the city's history, and by 1860 commercial and manufacturing areas as well as a central business district could be discerned.

In the 1830's and '40's commercial activity clustered along the Milwaukee River, particularly near its confluence with the Menomonee. Here was the naturally protected harbor area and here the earliest railroads brought grain for transshipment on the Great Lakes. Light manufacturing plants clustered along the banks, particularly at the lower end on the east side.

In the 1840's a second commercial district emerged along the Milwaukee River about a mile north of the earlier district. The attraction was a dam which Byron Kilbourn and other west-side promoters

---

8 Milw. Chamber of Commerce, 1875: p. 17; Milw. Chamber of Commerce, 1888: p. 47; Still, 1948: chs. 3, 8, and 13; Walsh, 1972: ch. 7; Whitbeck, 1921: pp. 84-101, 186-187; Derby, 1963: pp. 289-291.

built across the river as part of an abortive canal building scheme. The dam provided a valuable power source and quickly became a focal point for flour mills and other processing manufacturers.[9]

Between the two commercial and processing concentrations a business and retailing district began to appear. Solomon Juneau, the primary east-side promoter, had established a trading post in his area as early as 1819, and attracted most of the early business activity. In the 1830's he also garnered the Court House for his side. During that decade the east side was the most populous section and clearly the center of business activity. But by the 1850's the west side had become the city's largest section and part of the retailing and business activity extended across the river.[10]

In the late nineteenth century, industrial activity solidified its hold on its two initial locations —near the confluence of the Milwaukee and Menomonee and along the Milwaukee near the dam, and also expanded and extended to new areas. The area around the dam remained a center of processing firms. The Pabst and the Joseph Schlitz Brewing companies, each with 1,800 employees in 1910, were both located nearby on the west side. Numerous mills and tanneries were also in the area. Around the confluence of the Milwaukee and Menomonee Rivers were many of the smaller factories, particularly apparel, boots and shoes, knitting, and printing firms.[11]

In the 1870's the city carried out major improvements to attract new industry. The "Menomonee Improvements," begun in 1869, added 13,700 linear feet of dockage by building several canals across the floor of the Menomonee Valley. The valley became a major site for lumber, brick, and coal yards, and in the 1880's, an increasing number of large factories located there. In the early twentieth century, the valley included the yards and shops of the Chicago, Milwaukee, and St. Paul Railroad (with over 5,500 workers, the city's largest single industrial employer). International Harvester (2,200 workers), Miller Brewing Co., and numerous other industrial firms were located in or along the banks of the valley.[12] It is hard to overemphasize the importance of the Menomonee Valley in the physical development and land use of the city.

---

9 Stefaniak, 1962: pp. 15-17. Only one and a half miles of canal were ever built; the site, now filled in, is Commerce Street.

10 Conzen, 1976: pp. 136-148; Milw. Dept. of City Development, 1962: insert maps.

11 Stefaniak, 1962: ch. 2; Korman, 1959: p. 100; Korman, 1967: ch. 1 ; U.S. Bureau of the Census, 1879; Wis. Bureau of Labor and Industrial Statistics, 1912: part VII.

12 U.S. Bureau of the Census, 1887: part 2, p. 665; Korman, 1967: pp. 17-20.

Cutting through the center of the city, it provided an early measure of industrial decentralization fronting the immediate downtown locations, while—and this is essential—preserving easy accessibility to a large work force.

The southern lake shore also developed as a near industrial and employment center in the late nineteenth century. The Bay View iron and steel mills in Ward 17 led the area's development. Improvements to the Kinnickinnic Creek and two lines of the Chicago and Northwestern Railroad provided necessary transportation facilities for a number of foundries and metal fabricators and processors.[13] A small industrial concentration also appeared in the early twentieth century in the far northwest corner of the city where the tracks of the Milwaukee Road cut through Wards 20 and 22.

FIG. 1. W. Wisconsin Avenue (previously Grand Avenue), retail business district with the bridge across the Milwaukee River in foreground, 1892. Source: Milw. Real Estate Board, 1892.

---

13 Still, 1948: pp. 337-340; Whitbeck, 1921: p. 111; Wis. Bureau of Labor and Industrial Statistics, 1912: part VII.

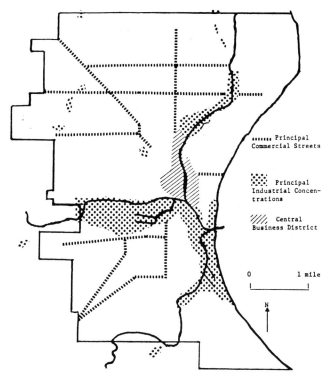

MAP. 2. Principal industrial and commercial districts of
Milwaukee, 1910. Sources: Wis. Bureau of Labor and
Industrial Statistics, 1912: part VII; Milw. Dept. of
City Development, 1962: insert maps.

FIG. 2. Milwaukee harbor looking south from Wisconsin Avenue, 1892. Source:
Milw. Real Estate Board, 1892.

In the late nineteenth century the central business district also expanded. Its major east-west axis was Wisconsin Avenue on both sides of the river. On the west side it had a north-south axis along Third Street, and on the east side it extended south from Wisconsin Avenue staying close to the river. With the electrification and extension of the streetcar in the 1890's a number of outlying streets also emerged as retailing locations: Third Street and Fond du Lac Avenue on the west side, North Avenue on the east side, and Muskego, Mitchell, and Lincoln Avenues on the south side. Map 2 shows the principal industrial and commercial districts of the city, the major retailing streets, and the location of the largest industrial employers in 1910.[14]

Several large manufacturing firms moved out of the city altogether, relocating in nearby towns. The largest of these firms founded their own industrial satellite towns around their plants. In 1893 the Patrick Cudahy Meatpacking Company moved southward to the town of Cudahy, and ten years later the E. P. Allis Company opened a new plant just to the west of the city limits in West Allis. Although most of the workers in the new industrial suburbs lived near the plants, Milwaukee continued to provide some of the labor force for those outlying factories which were connected to the city by streetcar lines.[15]

TRANSPORTATION

To cope with the surging population growth of the late nineteenth century, Milwaukee expanded its physical boundaries in all possible directions. The expansion was feasible, in part, because of the extension of the mass transportation system. Persons could now move three or four miles from the central business district and commute to work in a reasonable time. Electrification of the system, begun in 1890, extended the potential area for new neighborhoods. However, the streetcar was less important in Milwaukee than it was in some other large cities; consequently its role in the sorting out and segregating of social groups would be less determinative. In 1902 Milwaukee ranked twenty-first among the twenty-three metropolitan areas in per capita streetcar rider-

14 *Wright's City Directory*, 1905: Business Directory; Milw. Dept. of City Development, 1962: insert maps.

15 McShane, 1975: p. 91; Still, 1948: pp. 379-380; Korman, 1959: pp. 47-48. In 1910 West Allis had 6,645 residents, but the five largest industrial firms employed 3,600 people. Clearly part of the town's work force lived in Milwaukee. Wis. Sec. of State, 1906: pp. 170, 350; Wis. Bureau of Labor and Industrial Statistics, 1912: part VII; U.S. Bureau of the Census, 1913: p. 75.

ship. Three factors account for Milwaukee's relatively low use of mass transportation.

First, the dispersion of employment along the lake shore and the Menomonee Valley enabled workers to live several miles from the central business district and still be within walking distance to major employment centers.

Second, Milwaukee was extremely compact in its development. Lots were small and there was little open space. Congestion was not intense within the dwellings, rather the land was densely built over. (Table 3 compares Milwaukee with the other cities of 200,000 or more by streetcar ridership, persons per acre, and persons per dwelling.)

Third, streetcar fares, while inexpensive, were still beyond the means of many unskilled workers. It was the growing middle class, the clerks, professionals, shopkeepers, and highly skilled craftsmen, who could best afford to use the streetcar for daily commuting. As already pointed out, Milwaukee's share of this sector of the work force was proportionately lower than in some other cities.[16] The streetcar network focused on the downtown area, as was typical of American cities, but it did not provide direct service from the outlying portions of the city to the Menomonee Valley. Nor was there any meaningful crosstown service because there was no bridge over the valley outside of the downtown area. There was one crosstown line connecting the east and west sides, along North Avenue, but it was built to provide access to several parks and the lake shore, and so offered poor service on weekdays.[17]

The importance of the streetcar for the process of urban growth lies in the location and timing of the extensions of specific routes, and the relationship between those extensions and the city-building process. In subsequent chapters those relationships are explored in detail.

HOUSING AND SERVICES

Creating new residential neighborhoods at the city's periphery meant adding to the housing stock and providing at least the basic services for convenience and health. The most essential of these were streets, water mains, and sewer lines. The municipality had virtually no involvement in the extension of the housing supply, but it did undertake to provide the services.

16 McShane, 1975: chs. 3 and 4; Ottensmann, 1975: pp. 35-36.

17 McShane, 1975: p. 102; Canfield, 1972: p. 26 and ch. 5; Reisser, 1977: pp. 28-29; Milw. Sentinel, Dec. 25, 1895.

The new housing built on the expanding periphery of the city was similar to that found in most middle-sized and middle-western American cities: single family detached frame cottages and double-decker two-family flats on long narrow lots. Between 1880 and 1910 the housing stock and the population grew in the same proportions, enabling the city to maintain its ratio of 6.2 persons and 1.3 families per dwelling. In 1900, 58 percent of the families lived in single-family dwellings. There

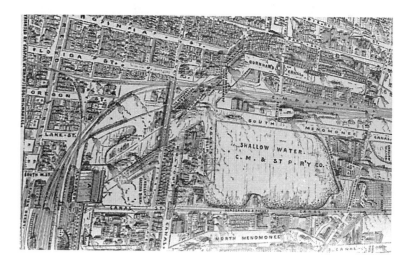

Fig. 3. View of the Menononee Valley looking west from Reed Street to Muskego Avenue, 1886. Source: Caspar and Zahn, 1886.

Fig. 4. East Side of central business district looking northeast from Wisconsin Avenue at Milwaukee River. Source: Milw. Real Estate Board, 1892.

were few "tenements" in the stereotyped sense of large multi-family structures and most of those were in the oldest part of the city. Row houses and "twins" (semidetached structures), were almost non-existent.[18] It was not until the 1870's that Milwaukee moved decisively to provide public water and sewer systems. The growing desire of middle-income homeowners to have indoor plumbing, the advances in public health and control of epidemics, and the devastation of the Chicago fire of 1871 combined with the steady increase of Milwaukee's population to stimulate community interest in supporting both of those services.[19]

18 U.S. Bureau of the Census, 1883: p. 670; U.S. Bureau of the Census, 1906: p. 732; U.S. Bureau of the Census, 1912: 1: p. 1289; U.S. Congress, Senate, 1911: pp. 266-267. A double-decker should not be confused with the "twin," or "semi-detached," found primarily in the northeast, particularly in the smaller cities. Both are two-family residences, but a twin is a modified form of row house and is split vertically, whereas a double-decker is split horizontally. The distinction is vital, because separate ownership is common with twins since separate title to the land is possible. With double-deckers (or the larger variant, triple-deckers) there is almost invariably just one owner.

19 Milw. Common Council, Select Committee in Relation to Water Works, n.d.; Milw. Board of Water Commissioners, 1873; Still, 1948: pp. 99, 247; Larson, 1908: pp. 108-112. For an extensive treatment of the sanitation and public health movement in Milwaukee, see Leavitt, 1975.

As the city enlarged its network of services, it managed to keep ahead of the net population increase. There was a surge of construction from the late 1880's through the mid-'90's. The activity was first stimulated by the real estate boom and heightened concern about public health, and then, as prosperity turned to depression, by work relief. Over the thirty-year period from 1880 to 1910 the ratio of persons and dwellings per water tap and sewer connection dropped steadily (table 4).

TABLE 3

STREETCAR RIDES PER INHABITANT AND DENSITY OF
CITIES OVER 200,000 IN 1910

Cities Ranked by Population, 1910[a]	Streetcar Rides per Inhabitant, 1902[b]	Rank	Persons per Acre, 1902[c]	Rank	Persons per Dwelling, 1900	Rank
NYC	266	2	17.3	8	13.7	1
Chi.	232	8*	14.9	14	8.8	2
Phil.	256	5	16.2	10	5.4	24*
St.L.	211	11	15.3	13	7.0	8*
Bstn.	246	6	21.4	2	8.4	4
Clvl.	201	12*	18.0	7	6.0	17
Balt.	190	14	27.1	1	5.7	20
Pitt.	263	3	18.6	5	6.3	14
Detr.	n.a.		17.2	9	5.5	22*
Buff.	176	17	13.8	16	7.1	7
S.F.	340	1	11.8	17	6.4	12*
Milw.	156	21	21.3	3	6.2	15*
Cinc.	201	12*	11.0	18	8.0	6
Nwrk.	153	22	18.3	6	8.1	5
N.O.	185	15	2.4	28	5.4	24*
Wash.	228	10	7.5	21	5.6	21
L.A.	259	4	4.0	26	4.5	28
Mpls.	166	20	6.2	22	6.4	12*
Jr.C.			20.6	4	8.7	3
K.C.	241	7	10.5	19	5.8	19
Sttl.	n.a.		4.4	25	6.8	10
Inpl.	177	16	10.3	20	4.7	27
Prov.	168	18*	15.8	12	7.0	8*
Loui.	168	18*	16.2	10	5.9	18
Roch.	113	24	14.2	15	5.5	22*
St.P.			4.8	24	6.6	11
Denv.	232	8*	3.6	27	4.9	26
Port.	n.a.		5.4	23	6.2	15*

ᵃ See table 2 for key to abbreviations.
ᵇ Based on metropolitan area population and traffic. Thus Minneapolis-St. Paul and Newark-Jersey City are combined.
ᶜ Based on population estimates made by Census Bureau.
* Tied for the same rank; rankings are only among cities listed in table.
n.a.—Not available.
Sources: U.S. Bureau of the Census, 1905: p. 24; 1904: pp. 6–12; 1912: 1: p. 1289.

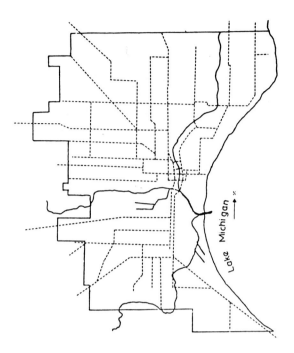

MAP. 3. Milwaukee streetcar routes, 1905.
Source: C. N. Caspar Co., 1905.

The Board of Public Works had responsibility for the water system, sewers, and streets. However, both the financing and the decision-making on extension of services were shared by the board and the property owner. The board planned and financed such general facilities as the pumping station, feeder mains, and the paving of main streets, but elsewhere abutting property owners paid an assessment for all or part of the cost of the improvement. In the case of sewer mains the abutter could be assessed no more than $.80 per front foot ($24.00 for the standard thirty-foot lot).[20]

The decision to extend the water and sewer systems to a particular block was, of course, partly a function of the current reach of the system. However, property owners could petition the board for new services, or conversely petition to delay a planned extension. An elaborate procedure was necessary to circumvent those requirements. In all cases, the Common Council, whose members were elected on a ward basis, had the

20 Wis., 1874: chs. V, VIII; Larson, 1908: p. 115; Leavitt, 1975: pp. 79-85, 188-190; Milw. Board of Public Works, 1893: pp. 5, 6, 12.

final say, but they did not usually impose their will on the owners.[21]

The extensions of the sewer and water systems helped to bring about a dramatic fall in mortality among Milwaukee citizens during the period. The decline in the death rate largely reflected nationwide and citywide advances in public health and the decline in infant mortality. In addition to the proliferation of water and sewer lines the city's health department aggressively tried to extend its jurisdiction and authority to eliminate health hazards. The era was marked by political struggles over a pure milk supply, garbage removal, inoculation and quarantining, and the elimination of privy vaults and private wells. Private citizens and businessmen often resisted public health measures which would raise their costs or their taxes. Such measures as inoculation, milk inspection, and the closing of privy vaults were also seen as violations of personal liberty and unwarranted extensions of public authority. Despite the protests, which were occasionally violent, the public health of the local community improved substantially.[22]

Not all sections of the city, however, enjoyed equally good health conditions. Overcrowding, inadequate diet, an unsatisfactory water supply, and ignorance of public health precautions certainly took their toll. Such conditions were not confined to the oldest houses in the inner wards. As table 5 shows, Ward 14, at the city's southwest periphery, sustained the highest crude death rate per thousand in 1910. The reasons for this condition are explored in chapter 4.

Nevertheless, Milwaukee was among the healthiest of the large American cities at the turn of the century, despite her density and her high percentage of children. (Nationally, in 1910, 27 percent of all deaths were among children under five). Milwaukee ranked twenty-third among the twenty-eight largest cities in crude death rate per thousand. Comparison of crude death rates is not the best measure of a city's sanitary conditions. The infant mortality rate (infant deaths per thousand live births) would be a superior indicator, but registration of births was so unreliable for the period that such statistics are lacking. The unhealthiest cities, New Orleans, Washington, and Baltimore, were all in the south and had a high percentage of blacks, a group with an astonishingly high death rate. But some northern industrial cities, Pittsburgh, Jersey City, Cincinnati, and Boston, also evidenced death

---

21 Wis., 1874: ch. VII, sec. 2, 6; Still, 1948: pp. 360-361; Larson, 1908: pp. 115-116; Milw. Common Council, MS. papers; compare with Lubove, 1969: p. 52.

22 Milw. Dept. of Health, 1891: pp. 29-30; Leavitt, 1975: passim.

rates well above the average for the period .[23]

POPULATION: COMPOSITION AND DISTRIBUTION

Milwaukee's population, like that of other rapidly growing cities in the nineteenth century, included large contingents of European immigrants. In 1880 just under 40 percent of all Milwaukeeans were foreign-born, over two-thirds of them from Germany. Ireland, a far distant second, provided almost 8 percent of the foreign-born, and Poland, then in third place, added another 4 percent. Measured by percentage of its population, Milwaukee had the fifth largest immigrant contingent among the fifty largest cities. Furthermore, the city's immigrant population was exceptionally homogeneous. Among the twenty largest cities in 1880, Milwaukee ranked first in percentage of total population born in a single foreign country: 27.2 percent of all Milwaukeeans were German-born.[24]

Throughout the next thirty years the number of immigrants in the city continued to rise, but not as fast as the population. By 1910 Milwaukee's foreign-born contingent was down to 30 percent, and yet Milwaukee in 1910 contained more persons of foreign birth than at any other time in her history. The most significant change that occurred in the immigrant population was the decline in the share of foreign-born of German origin. The foreign stock of German extraction in 1910 accounted for 44.8 percent of the total population of the city.[25] The population of Polish stock, although only a third as large, added a whole new element to the city's ethnic structure after 1880. The Poles constituted a fifth of the total foreign-born population in 1910. Although the census did not indicate particular foreign-born groups by year of arrival it is likely that the Poles accounted for a much higher percentage of the recent arrivals.

A comparison of Milwaukee's foreign-born population with that of other large cities indicates the relatively small degree to which she shared in the "new immigration" of the early twentieth century. Although Milwaukee dropped from fifth to ninth in rank by percentage of

---

23 U.S. Bureau of the Census, 1912c: p. 12; U.S. Bureau of the Census, 1913: pp. 139-145.

24 Galford, 1957: pp. 232-234, 242; Still, 1948: pp. 262-272; Conzen, 1976: ch. 1 provides an excellent discussion of the early immigration to the city.

25 Foreign stock includes persons, whether native or foreign born, with at least one foreign-born parent.

TABLE 4

EXPANSION OF THE WATER AND SEWER NETWORK, AND CRUDE DEATH RATE, MILWAUKEE, 1880–1910

	1880	1885	1890	1895	1900	1905	1910
Miles of Water Mains	91	121	190	292	345	397	463
Per cent Increase in Water Mains		32.6	57.7	53.9	17.9	15.1	16.6
Persons per Water Tap	16.8	n.a.	12.0	8.4	6.9	6.0	5.8
Dwellings per Water Tap	2.7	n.a.	1.9	n.a.	1.1	n.a.	1.3
Miles of Sewer Mains	98	127	196	284	328	374	428
Per cent Increase in Sewer Mains		29.6	53.5	45.6	15.5	14.0	14.4
Persons per Sewer Connection	n.a.	n.a.	12.0	8.6	n.a.	6.8	6.7
Dwellings per Sewer Connection	n.a.	n.a.	1.9	n.a.	n.a.	n.a.	1.4
Crude Death Rate, per Thousand	20.68	17.92	18.33	15.54	13.88	12.19	13.90

n.a.—Not available.
Sources: Milw. Dept. of Public Works, 1881; 1886; 1891; 1896; 1901; 1906; 1911; Milw. Dept. of Health. 1911: pp. 43–44.

foreign-born population, she was tied for first in percentage of population of foreign stock. With almost half of her citizens of German extraction, Milwaukee continued to be the country's most ethnically homogeneous large city.[26]

The influence of the overwhelmingly large German population on Milwaukee's cultural life and subsequently its politics was profound. The impact on the economy and other aspects of the city's development was less clear. Kathleen Conzen has argued that the large German community eased that group's adjustment to a new culture. It provided ample entrepreneurial opportunity for its members, but may also have served to delay acculturation and assimilation. German traditions and cultural norms certainly received considerable reinforcement in nineteenth-century Milwaukee.[27]

Conzen pointed out two characteristic traits of the German community that may have influenced the housing stock of the city. The first was the central role of the family unit. The German migration was largely a "migration in families." There were fewer single men among the German immigrants than in most other ethnic groups. Socializing among family members and relatives also played a major role in the recreational life of the German community. Second, Germans seemed to have a greater tendency or preference for homeownership than other groups.

It is not clear, however, to what extent these important traits were really disproportionate among the Germans. In 1900, for the country as a whole, a higher percentage of non-farm families of German extraction were homeowners than any other ethnic group, including native-stock whites. In Milwaukee, however, Germans and Poles, most of whom were from the German section, were virtually tied for first place in percentage of private families owning homes. Our knowledge of ethnic differences is inadequate as yet to indicate precisely the influence that a particular ethnic composition might have had on a given city. The detailed analysis of different neighborhoods, which follows, will shed some light on this issue.[28]

The large immigrant population was not distributed equally throughout the city; rather, from its earliest days new arrivals had commonly sought out fellow countrymen and clustered in distinct areas of the city.

---

26 U.S. Bureau of the Census, 1912: 1: pp. 178, 826, 828, 1007; Still, 1974: pp. 264-267.

27 Conzen, 1976: pp. 1-9, 153, 156.

28 Conzen, 1976: pp. 51-52, 55, 60-61, 77-80. It is particularly difficult to separate the ethnic from the class dimension. U.S. Bureau of the Census, 1902: 2: pp. 742, 752.

The patterns of segregation established at the outset perpetuated themselves over several generations.[29]

By the 1850's, the Irish, over half of whom were unskilled laborers, clustered south of the emergent business district on the east side. That area was close to the commercial port facilities, providing them with job opportunities. More affluent groups shunned the lower portion of the east side, at first because it was low and swampy, and then because the Irish were there. East of the emerging central business district, and north of the Irish, was Milwaukee's most fashionable neighborhood from the 1850's through the early twentieth century. The early residents were primarily Yankees and British immigrants. The area had the distinct advantage of easy access to the business center in an era when almost everyone walked to work, and further, it was high and dry. Along the lake shore rose the imposing bluffs which provided attractive home sites.

Milwaukee's already dominant German population could be found everywhere, but they virtually took over the west side for themselves and created there, in the third quarter of the nineteenth century, a largely self-contained microcosm of the whole city. The south side showed less dominance by a single ethnic group, although Germans did tend to cluster in the more westerly part of the section. Land values and public esteem rated the south side lower than the other sections of the city which made it attractive for the immigrant working class.[30]

In the early twentieth century the sorting out process continued to separate the population along several dimensions. We can measure the magnitude and direction of this segregation in two ways. The first measure, the index of dissimilarity, is a city-wide indicator of segregation. The index number is actually the percentage of one group that would have to be moved to another ward to eliminate any segregation at the ward level. Two groups, Poles and non-Poles, for example, would be considered fully integrated if every ward had the same percentage of the city's population of Poles and of non-Poles. The second index, the index of disproportion or segregation, is a ward measure showing whether a given group is over-or underrepresented in a ward, relative to its proportion of the total population of the city. For example, if 10 percent of the city's population was Polish-born, and Poles were not at all segregated by ward, then 10 percent of each ward's population would be Polish. The index of disproportion for each ward would be 100. But, if a given ward

---

29 Conzen, 1976: pp. 126-153; Still, 1948: pp. 269, 271, 276; Korman, 1967: ch. 2.

30 Still, 1948: 396-397; Sanborn and Perris Map Co., 1894.

TABLE 5

HOUSING AND HEALTH STATISTICS OF MILWAUKEE WARDS,
1910, BY DISTANCE FROM THE CENTER

	Per cent of Homes Rented	Persons per Dwelling	Families per Dwelling	Crude Death Rate per 1,000
Central Business District				
2	84.4	7.18	1.58	11.73
3	88.7	10.07	1.78	12.00
4	87.0	7.85	1.50	12.66
7	83.6	7.86	1.60	8.43
Intermediate East				
1	71.7	6.09	1.35	11.30
West				
6	74.0	5.83	1.30	11.56
9	71.6	6.30	1.40	10.81
10	66.6	5.87	1.39	10.16
13	61.4	5.91	1.35	10.65
South				
5	76.6	6.20	1.20	11.64
8	71.4	5.32	1.20	10.80
12	69.0	6.45	1.31	11.37
Peripheral East				
18	56.5	6.07	1.28	12.58
West				
15	65.9	5.12	1.22	10.93
16	64.4	6.01	1.24	14.41
19	56.2	5.57	1.32	13.33
20	49.2	5.35	1.22	11.73
21	50.4	5.57	1.41	12.61
22	53.0	5.65	1.28	11.82
South				
11	55.0	6.43	1.31	11.66
14	53.6	8.96	1.59	15.73
17	56.2	6.06	1.23	11.93
23	57.0	5.23	1.21	12.33

Sources: U.S. Bureau of the Census, 1912: 1: p. 1366;
1912*d*: p. 621; Milw. Dept. of Health, 1911: p. 45.

Fig. 5. Typical cottages of German artisans on Milwaukee's northwest side, 1905.
Source: Wis. Bureau of Labor and Industrial Statistics, 1906: illustration six.

were 20 percent Polish, its index value would then be 200; if it were 5 percent Polish, the index value would be 50.[31]

The city's largest ethnic group, the Germans, was so overwhelming in number that it could be found in every ward and by 1910 was not highly segregated. Nevertheless, as map 4 shows, the Germans were still disproportionately clustered in the west side, which they had dominated since the 1840's. For the most part this was an area of one- and two-story detached frame homes sitting on long narrow blocks. Except near the central business district most of these homes were built after the Civil War and hence still considered fairly new. The two most peripheral wards in this section, Wards 20 and 22, are examined in depth in Chapter 3.

Polish immigrants continued to cluster in two areas. By far the largest area was on the south side in Wards 11, 12, and 14. In 1905 Ward 14 contained over 53 percent of all the German-Poles in Milwaukee. The typical dwelling here was a one-story cottage. The cottage

---

31 For a comprehensive discussion of the index of dissimilarity and other indices of segregation, see Taeuber and Taeuber, 1969: pp. 195-245. For recent applications by historians, see Warner, 1968: pp. 13, 170, 226-227; Chudacoff, 1972: pp. 65-68; Conzen, 1976: pp. 130, 137.

started out as a four-room dwelling which, on occasion, housed two families. As the owner continued to save, he often added a basement or raised the older dwelling and built a new first floor. The basement was then usually rented out to a second family to help with the mortgage. Later, when the house was free of debt, the owner would often take over the entire dwelling. Such a system eventually enabled many Polish immigrants and their sons to own their own homes, but meanwhile it led to some of the worst housing conditions in the city. The basement or semibasement dwelling units which abounded in Wards 11, 12, and 14 were damp, dark, and often dirty. The 1910 Basement Tenements survey provided a vivid description of conditions on the south side:

> From the northeast corner of the 12th Ward ... southwest to Forest Home Avenue on each side of every street or avenue is an almost continuous line of basements, miles and miles of gloomy, poorly lighted, damp, unventilated, overcrowded rooms. . . . They are nearly all less than 8 feet from floor to ceiling, nearly all less than 4 feet above the ground. They either have less than 1/10 of the floor area represented in window space, or the windows are obstructed by other houses. They are mostly damp and if old are filthy and in ill repair, and invariably poorly ventilated.[32]

The investigators reported that the homes in Ward 14, because they were newer, were less congested and disease-ridden. Nevertheless, they found that bedrooms with sufficient air space for two adults often accommodated four persons and an infant. They also found that it was a habit among the Polish immigrants to admit as little fresh air as possible. Chickens, ducks, geese, and goats also inhabited the ward in some number and dogs appeared to be "almost indispensable." Since the landlord usually lived on the premises and rented only half the dwelling to meet his payments, the houses were usually in good repair.[33]

Ward 14 had the highest density in the city, 36 persons per acre, and the highest local death rate, 15.1 per thousand. Although most of the dwelling units in the ward had separate water supplies, separate toilet facilities were rare. On a "typical" but unspecified block in the ward, investigators classified 26 of 44 dwellings in "good sanitary condition" and only 3 in bad condition, yet, they found plumbing facilities in only 21 of the dwellings. The basements of all but 6 of the 44 dwellings were

---

32 Wis. Bureau of Labor and Industrial Statistics, 1914: pp. 173-174; Milw. Commissioner of Health, 1916: p. 12; see also Thompson, 1910.

33 Wis. Bureau of Labor and Industrial Statistics, 1914: p. 177.

TABLE 6

COMPOSITION OF FOREIGN-BORN POPULATION
OF MILWAUKEE, 1880–1910

	1880	1890	1900	1905	1910
Total Foreign Born (1,000's)	46.1	79.6	89.0	95.2	111.5
Per cent of Foreign Born by Selected Countries of Origin[a]					
England–Scotland–Wales	5.5	4.3	3.6	2.3	2.7
Ireland	7.9	4.3	3.0	2.7	1.8
Canada	2.1	1.6	2.1	1.9	1.7
Germany	68.3	68.8	60.5	57.1	58.1
Norway–Sweden–Denmark	3.1	3.1	3.2	2.2	3.2
Austria	2.1	1.2	1.8	2.7	10.4
Hungary	0.2	0.3	0.4	1.5	5.0
Bohemia	3.3	1.8	2.0	2.1	n.a.
Poland (Unspecified)[b]	3.9	11.6	0.1	0	n.a.
Poland (German)	n.a.	n.a.	17.0	16.0	n.a.
Poland (Russian)	n.a.	n.a.	1.4	1.4	n.a.
Poland (Austrian)	n.a.	n.a.	0.7	0.6	n.a.
Russia[c]	0.2	0.7	1.3	2.4	10.9
Italy	0.2	0.2	0.8	0.6	3.0

Per cent of Foreign Born by Mother Tongue, 1910		Per cent of Foreign Born by Year of Arrival	
German	49.8	1890 or before	52.6
Polish	21.8	1891–1895	10.5
English	5.7	1896–1900	4.3
Yiddish	4.7	1901–1905	13.1
All Scandinavian	3.2	1906–4/15/1910	19.6
Italian	3.0		
Bohemian	2.5		

[a] The U.S. census of 1880, 1890, and 1900, and the Wisconsin census of 1905 considered Poland and Bohemia as separate countries. The 1900 and 1905 census further specified whether the Poles came from lands under the German, Russian, or Austrian Empires. The 1910 census only recognized political jurisdictions as countries. This accounts for the sharp rise in the number of Austrians and Russians and the stability of the Germans between 1905 and 1910 in the table. The 1910 census did include questions on the mother tongue of the foreign-born which is a reasonable indication of the number of Poles in Milwaukee in that year. For the country as a whole in 1910, 7.6 per cent of the German-born, 28.0 percent of the Austrian-born, and 26.1 per cent of the Russian-born listed Polish as their mother tongue.

[b] Also includes Polish, unknown.

[c] Includes Finland for 1910.

n.a.—Not available.

Sources: U.S. Bureau of the Census, 1883: pp. 538–541; 1895: pp. 800–803; 1912: 1: pp. 98, 826, 828, 1023; 1913: p. 193; Wis. Sec. of State, 1906: pp. 170–173.

TABLE 7

INDEX OF DISSIMILARITY OF FOREIGN-BORN FROM
BALANCE OF POPULATION, 1905

Group	Index	Per cent of Total Foreign-Born[a]
Italians	79	1.4
Poles (Germany)[b]	67	16.0
Russians	60	2.4
Norwegians	58	2.3
Poles (Austria)[b]	55	0.6
Hungarians	51	1.5
Bohemians	51	2.2
Irish	50	2.3
Poles (Russia)[b]	48	2.7
Canadians	37	1.9
Austrians	33	2.7
English	33	2.1
Germans	22	57.1

[a] The above groups account for 95.2 per cent of the foreign-born in 1905.

[b] Germany, Austria, and Russia refer to the sectors of Poland controlled by those respective countries. See note to table 6.

Source: Wis. Sec. of State, 1906: p. 36.

used as habitations; 11 of these basement families lived in one room.[34] The development of Ward 14 will be analyzed in Chapter 4.

A smaller Polish community straddled the dam across the Milwaukee River. Conditions in that area were even worse than on the south side. The Immigration Commission described the rear dwellings, which were common in the Polish area, as being

for the most part, in much worse repair than the front house. With but three or four exceptions they are little one-story frame cottages of two, sometimes three, very small rooms. The foundations are in many cases of wooden piles which have settled unevenly and left the floors and roof sagging. Only six out of the 31 rear houses have water supply or toilet within the house; the tenants in the rear houses on each of the other lots use in common a hydrant in the yard, and the toilet in the basement of the front house or a dry toilet in the Yard.[35]

---

34 Wis. Bureau of Labor and Industrial Statistics, 1906: part IV, pp. 312-315; U.S. Congress, Senate, 1911: pp. 265-266.

35 U.S. Congress, Senate, 1911a: 1: p. 688; U.S. Bureau of the Census, 1913a: pp. 68, 73, 148, 154.

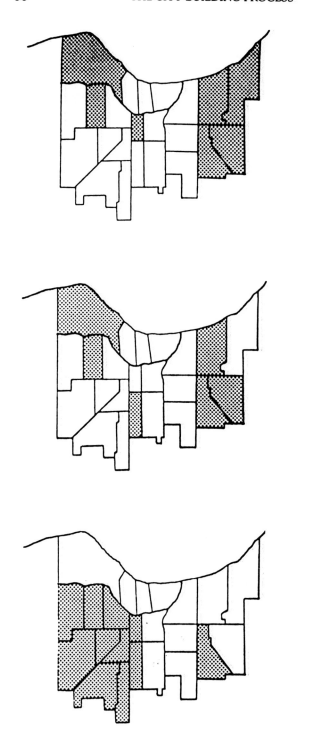

GERMAN—BORN   GERMAN—POLISH—BORN   RUSSIAN—POLISH—BORN

MAP. 4. Milwaukee in 1905 showing wards with overrepresentation of German-, German-Polish-, and Russian-Polish-born persons. Shaded wards contained an overrepresentation of indicated group. Source: Wis. Sec. of State, 1906: pp. 171–173.

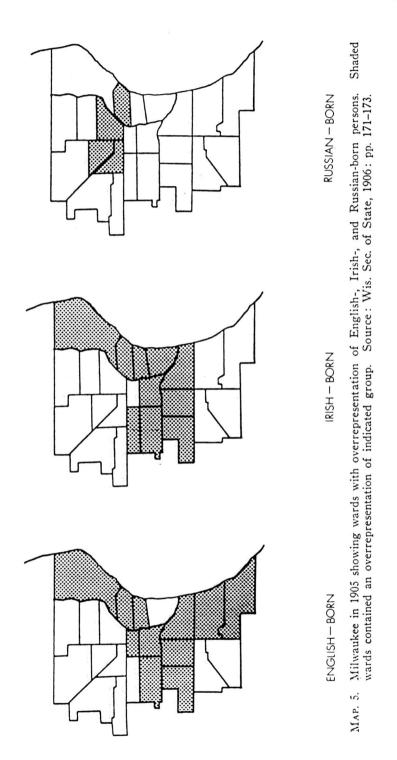

ENGLISH—BORN

IRISH—BORN

RUSSIAN—BORN

MAP. 5. Milwaukee in 1905 showing wards with overrepresentation of English-, Irish-, and Russian-born persons. Shaded wards contained an overrepresentation of indicated group. Source: Wis. Sec. of State, 1906: pp. 171-173.

Although there was adequate yard space to provide sufficient light and air, the grounds generally contained more rubbish than grass and were incredibly muddy in wet weather.

The smaller group of eastern and southern European immigrants—Italians, Russians, Hungarians, Jews, and Slovaks—did follow the pattern found among similar groups in older eastern cities. They lived around the edges of the expanding central business district in what was by 1900 an old and deteriorated housing stock. The Italians, the single most segregated immigrant group in the city, clustered in Ward 3, where they had succeeded the earlier Irish immigrants. Here were to be found employment opportunities in the warehouses and docks, as well as Catholic churches. Most of the small tenement houses that did exist in Milwaukee were located in that area; there were a few instances of four narrow tenements on a single lot.[36]

The smaller East European groups clustered in Wards, 2, 6, 9, and 13 on the west side. Here were located the retail portions of the business district and most of the processing and fabricating plants. Farther from the dock area, it was closer to the Menomonee Valley. It was the area of first-generation German settlement. By 1900 it was overcrowded, but conditions were not as serious as in Ward 3. Most dwelling units had their own separate water supplies, usually the kitchen sinks, although private toilet facilities were less widespread, and frequently were found in the basements.[37] The English and Irish immigrants displayed another pattern. Both groups clustered around the Menomonee Valley and along the eastern lake shore. The English still clustered near the iron and machinery plants on the southern lake shore. The configurations reflect the concentration of the English in skilled mechanical crafts, in positions as foremen, and among the fashionable socioeconomic groups that gravitated towards the northern lake shore, in Wards 1, 7, and 18. (Ward 18 will be examined in Chapter 5.) The Irish also clustered around the railroad yards in the valley, but their clustering near the lake shore reflected their continuing duties as domestic servants more than an arrival among the socially elite.

The population was less residentially segregated by occupation than by ethnicity, despite the tendency of particular ethnic groups to

---

36 Wis. Bureau of Labor and Industrial Statistics, 1906: pp. 292-293; Wis. Bureau of Labor and Industrial Statistics, 1914: pp. 15-52, 149-150; U.S. Congress, Senate, 1911a: 1 : p. 688.

37 Wis. Bureau of Labor and Industrial Statistics, 1915: p. 183; U.S. Congress, Senate, 1911a: 1 : pp. 683-684, 689.

concentrate in certain occupations. Table 8 shows the index of dissimilarity for selected occupational groups in 1905 by ward. The highest
levels of segregation were in those occupations requiring the most or the
least skill. Between a fifth and a quarter of the physicians, teachers, and
other professionals would have to be moved for those groups to be
distributed, by ward, in equal proportions to the rest of the population.
A quarter of all unskilled workers and almost the same percentage of
servants would have to be moved to eliminate spatial segregation. The
lowest indices of dissimilarity by wards occurred among the skilled
artisans.

Fig. 6. Typical Ward 14 block, 1905. Source: Wis. Bureau of Labor and Industrial
Statistics, 1906: illustration xviii.

Fig. 7. Fashionable Prospect Avenue in Ward 1 on the east side, 1892. Source:
Milw. Real Estate Board, 1892.

TABLE 8

INDEX OF DISSIMILARITY OF OCCUPATIONAL GROUPS FROM
BALANCE OF WORK FORCE, MILWAUKEE, 1905

Occupation	Index of Dissimilarity	Per cent of Total Work Force
All Unskilled, except		
Servants	25	25.4
Servants	24	4.7
All Professionals	23	6.0
Railroad Workers	23	3.5
Agents and Clerks	21	19.1
Metal Workers	20	5.7
Foremen	19	1.2
Building Tradesmen	18	7.4
Stationary Engineers	15	4.6
Tailors	14	5.5
Other Skilled Workers	13	10.8
Proprietors	13	7.5

Source: Wis. Sec. of State, 1906: pp. 447–451.

Somewhat higher levels of segregation were revealed when we compare the dissimilarity of two occupational groups from one another. Table 9 shows these indices. By computing the segregation measures in this way, we find several clusters of occupations which displayed little segregation among themselves, and yet were much more segregated from other occupational groups. Thus professionals, proprietors, agents and clerks, and servants (largely in residence in this period) showed little segregation from one another, as did stationary engineers, foremen and railroad workers. Building tradesmen and other skilled workers were also little segregated from each other. The highest levels of segregation were between unskilled labors and metal workers, on the one hand, and professionals, proprietors, agents, and servants on the other.

The striking aspect of the spatial distribution of the work force was the clustering of the professional and white-collar groups in the central business district and in those wards with most convenient access to it (map 6). The professional group as a whole clustered on the east side in Wards 1, 7, and 18, on the west side in Wards 4, 15, and 16, and only in Ward 5 on the south side, which was adjacent to the central business district. Physicians and teachers both concentrated in wards either directly west or directly northeast of the business district. The distribution of

TABLE 9

INDICES OF DISSIMILARITY OF OCCUPATIONAL GROUPS FROM EACH OTHER, MILWAUKEE, 1905

	Professionals	Proprietors	Agents, Clerks	Servants	Foremen	Railroad Workers	Metal Workers	Stationary Engineers	Building Tradesmen	Other Skilled Workers
Proprietors	17									
Agents, Clerks	15	8								
Servants	16	19	18							
Foremen	22	21	18	26						
Railroad Workers	23	21	22	23	20					
Metal Workers	31	29	31	40	28	33				
Stationary Engineers	29	20	22	31	19	18	23			
Building Tradesmen	34	25	25	38	27	33	22	22		
Other Skilled	28	19	19	34	27	32	24	22	14	
Unskilled Workers	38	29	32	38	31	33	15	21	24	24

Source: Wis. Sec. of State, 1906: pp. 447–451.

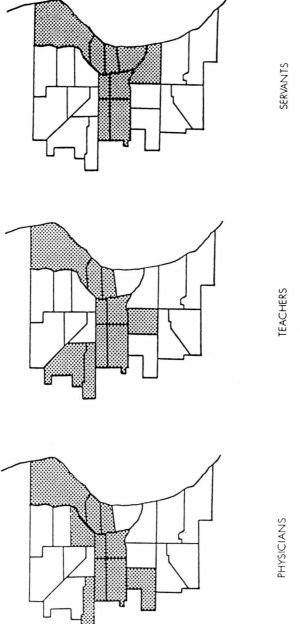

PHYSICIANS   TEACHERS   SERVANTS

MAP. 6. Milwaukee in 1905 showing wards with overrepresentation of physicians, teachers, and servants. Shaded wards contained an overrepresentation of indicated group. Source: Wis. Sec. of State, 1906: pp. 447–451.

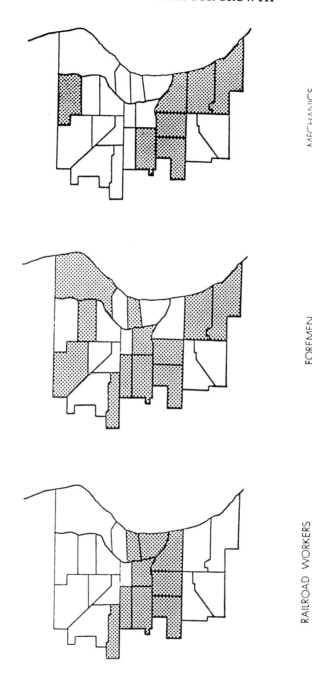

RAILROAD WORKERS   FOREMEN   MECHANICS

MAP. 7. Milwaukee in 1905 showing wards with overrepresentation of railroad workers, foremen, and mechanics. Shaded wards contained an overrepresentation of indicated group. Source: Wis. Sec. of State, 1906: pp. 447–451.

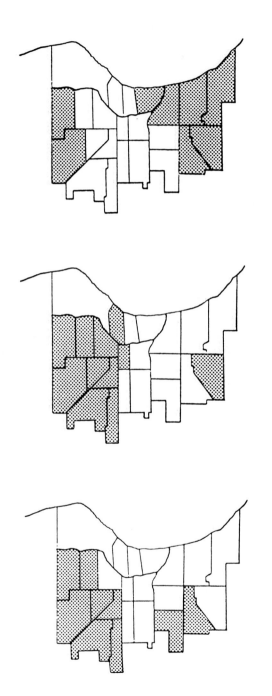

BUILDING TRADESMAN   OTHER SKILLED WORKERS   UNSKILLED WORKERS

MAP. 8. Milwaukee in 1905 showing wards with overrepresentation of building tradesmen, other skilled workers, and unskilled workers. Shaded wards contained an overrepresentation of indicated group. Source: Wis. Sec. of State, 1906: pp. 447–451.

servants in the same areas further indicates the location of the more fashionable residential areas. The highest concentrations of servants were in Wards 4 and 7. Proprietors displayed the same general pattern as professionals, although they were most overrepresented in Ward 15.

Clerical workers of all types showed patterns similar to professionals, not so much because of their incomes, although their job status was generally more secure than that of blue-collar workers, but because their employment was centered much more heavily in the central business district than was that of blue-collar workers. The distribution of foremen indicated an overlap of several trends. Foremen congregated near the major industrial installations of Ward 17 and the Menomonee Valley, but also, as befit their status and incomes, clustered in Wards 7 and 18.

Urban scholars have devoted considerable attention to the spatial distribution of the wealthiest segment of the population. In the pre-industrial era it was clearly advantageous to be centrally located, since most everyone walked about the city. Warner and others have argued that the wealthier segments of the population availed themselves of the opportunity to escape the growing pollution and the immigrants by suburbanizing with the assistance of the streetcar. Although this process did eventually occur in Milwaukee, the city in 1905 still held a disproportionate share of its professionals, proprietors, and white-collar workers in central locations.[38]

Skilled artisans were overrepresented in a contiguous block of wards encompassing the entire northwest section of the city, and around the Menomonee Valley. Particular skilled groups showed variations that conformed closely to the requirements of the trade. Blacksmiths, metal workers, stationary engineers, and machinists clustered around the valley and the industrial belt along the southern lake shore (map 7).

Railroad, telegraphy, and telephone workers were overrepresented in wards near the terminals, shops, and yards of the Milwaukee Road (Ward 16), and the Chicago and Northwestern (Wards 3 and 7). Railroads crisscrossed the entire floor of the valley and the distribution of railroad workers clustered accordingly.

Carpenters and other building tradesmen clustered around the periphery of the city and split into two communities. Thus the skilled building tradesmen could be found in the sections of the city where the greatest volume of new construction occurred. The major physical

---

38 Sjoberg, 1965: ch. 4, see esp. pp. 97-98; Schnore, 1965: chs. 11 and 12; Schnore, 1965a: pp. 347-398. The location of the wealthy was a major segment of the urban models of Burgess, 1924, and Hoyt, 1939; see also Hoyt, 1966.

barrier of the city, the Menomonee Valley, was suffiicent to cause the emergence of two distinct peripheral settlements of this occupational group, as with other segments of the work force.

Finally, the unskilled laborers were the most concentrated occupational group in the city. They tended to cluster in industrial areas and at the periphery. The overrepresentation of laborers in Ward 3 reflected the predominant Italian neighborhood there. Wards 5, 12, and 17 on the south side were centers of heavy industry, and, therefore, major sources of employment for the unskilled. Ward 11 was on the streetcar link to West Allis. Ward 14, with the highest concentration of the unskilled, also housed over half of the city's Polish immigrants. It was a peripheral ward with lower land values, but was still close enough for workers to walk north to the valley or east to the packing and iron plants along the lake. Two factors account for the slight concentration of unskilled laborers in the far northwest side in Wards 20 and 21. Since the area was peripheral, land values were lower than in more central locations; further, some manufacturing firms already were locating along the tracks of the Milwaukee Road in the western part of Ward 20, and those of the Chicago and Northwestern near the west bank of the Milwaukee River in Ward 21 (map 8).

Patterns of residential distribution are affected by variables other than socioeconomic class and cultural affinity. The stage in a family life cycle, for example, is a leading determinant of the housing needs of any particular family.[39] Within a relatively homogeneous ethnic or class area, family age and size may have been the most powerful force determining family location and the allocation of the housing stock. Unfortunately, aggregate data showing the spatial distribution of the population by family size do not exist, but we do know the spatial distribution of children of school age and we can compute indices of dissimilarity and disproportion. The index of dissimilarity for school-age children in 1905 was 14; in other words, 14 percent of those children would have to be moved to other wards for the children to be evenly distributed. This is not an exceptionally high degree of maldistribution, but school-age children were such a large proportion of the entire population (34 percent) that extensive segregation is not to be expected. Equally important, however, is the location and pattern of the maldistribution. Map 9 shows the index of disproportion for school-age children for each ward. Only the peripheral wards displayed an overrepresentation and the

---

39 For a discussion of this relationship, see Rossi, 1955, and Chudacoff, 1972: ch. 4.

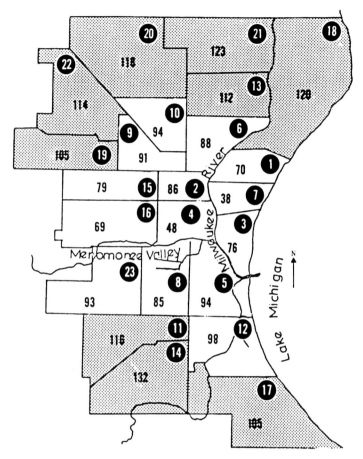

MAP. 9. Milwaukee in 1905 showing wards with overrepresentation of children of school age with index of disproportion. Source: Milw. Board of School Commissioners,
1905: p. 138.

the share of school-age children dropped steadily and regularly as one
approached the center of the city. The peripheral wards, most recently
built and still with considerable open space, featured a housing stock
with the most room both inside and outside the dwelling. Clearly there
was an association between the availability of more spacious quarters and
the location of families with growing children.

MILWAUKEE IN CONTEXT

A higher proportion of Milwaukee's suburbanites were workers'
families and immigrants than was the case in most older and larger

cities. Milwaukee in 1880 did not have a substantial stock of old housing that the emerging white-collar and lower-middle-class citizens could pass on to lower income families. In the thirty years after 1880 new housing had to be built for working-class families because the outward movement of the wealthier segment of the population alone would not leave behind enough shelter—even with multiple occupancy—for the larger, less affluent segment. To that extent Milwaukee was probably fairly typical of a group of Great Lakes and middlewestern cities that had grown from the 100,000 class to the 500,000 class by 1910. Cities such as Detroit, Cleveland, Buffalo, and Minneapolis-St. Paul all went through similar experiences in population growth and economic development at that time. The older, larger cities of the eastern seaboard, while sustaining significant growth rates in the same period and adding larger absolute numbers of citizens to their populations, already had a much larger and more diversified stock of housing than any of the cities noted above. In the middle west, meanwhile, Cincinnati, St. Louis, and Chicago were already considerably larger than Milwaukee by 1880. The point, of course, is not that the findings for Milwaukee can be applied indiscriminately to Cleveland, Buffalo, Minneapolis, or Detroit. Only when we know more about the influence of such variables as city age, residential density, ethnic, occupational, and family structure, and journey to work, among others, can we begin to compare the patterns of one city to any other.

3. FLATS AND COTTAGES IN THE NORTHWEST CORNER

IN 1905 Herman Ihbe lived with his wife and four children in a new cottage in Ward 20 on Milwaukee's northwest side. Ihbe was a forty-four-year-old German-born painter. His small home, which measured only 22 feet by 32 feet in exterior dimensions, cost about $1,600, and Ihbe had assumed a mortgage to purchase it. Ihbe's modest home probably gave him considerable satisfaction as well as some room for his growing family. His children could attend public school four blocks away, and his street had a water main and a sewer line which he could tap. The houses were packed tightly together, but the density was typical of the new blocks emerging in Ward 20.

A few streets to the north at 3056 N. 27th Street, Adolph Zebolski lived with his family of six in a new two-story home. Zebolski was a thirty-one-year-old molder, born in Wisconsin of German-born parents. His mortgaged home was one of nine identical houses that A. Klug, a small-scale real estate promoter, built in 1904. The dimensions of these dwellings were 24 by 38 feet and they cost about $2,000 each. All of Zebolski's neighbors in 1905 were of German or Swiss extraction and all were either skilled artisans or petty proprietors. Although the nearest public school was almost a mile away, Zebolski and his neighbors did have access to the city water and sewer systems.

The large two-family flat at 2047 N. 27th Street in Ward 22 was typical of a style being built in increasing numbers in early twentieth-century Milwaukee. The house, built in 1905, cost $4,000 and measured 24 by 56 feet. At the time of the state census only one unit was occupied; it was rented by Ulysses Bauman, a twenty-six-year-old cashier, and head of a family of four. Bauman was born in Iowa of parents who originated in Germany and Wisconsin. When he moved into his new home, he found that his street already included water and sewer mains and had gravel pavement and a sidewalk. His children could walk two blocks to primary school. If Bauman worked at a downtown bank or commercial firm he could catch a streetcar in front of his door.

In 1905 Fred Winkel operated a grocery store at the corner of 23rd and Hadley Streets in Ward 20. He had built the store, with an apartment above, in 1890, at a cost of $1,600. In 1899 he built a house next to the store for $3,000. It was a large two-story home, measuring 28 by 46 feet, and it housed six people. Winkel was Wisconsin-born as were

Fig. 8. 1820 W. Clarke Street, residence of Herman Ihbe in 1905. Picture, 1994, adjacent house on right demolished between 1974 and 1994.

Fig. 9. 3056 N. 27th Street, residence of Adolph Zebolski, 1905. Picture, 1974.

Fig. 10. 2045-47 N. 27th Street, residence of Ulysses Bauman, 1905. Picture, 1974.

Fig. 11. 2811 N. 23rd Street, residence of Fred Winkel, 1905. Picture, 1974.

his parents, although most of his neighbors, living in rather small one-story cottages, were German-born artisans. Winkel had a mortgage on his home in 1905, but in addition to his store and home, he owned three other house lots on the block, one of which contained two dwellings. Winkel was typical of the small builder who speculated in a few lots close to his own residence.

These families and dwellings are examples of the culmination of a process of city-building which, in some cases, spanned half a century from farm to finished street. How that process unfolded on the city's northwest side and how the resultant housing stock was allocated is the focus of this chapter.

The process of creating new urban neighborhoods consisted of four distinct elements: dividing the land for urban use, providing the basic services, creating a stock of housing, and populating the area. The completion of one component was not necessarily a prerequisite to the next, so there was considerable overlap in the stages of the process. The needs, aspirations, and financial abilities of the subdividers, the builders, the city, and the new residents all influenced the speed of the process and the quality of the resultant environments. The framework within which the subdividers and builders made their decisions lay in the social and economic characteristics of the population most likely to move into the area.

The expansion of Milwaukee in the northwest occurred on relatively open, unsettled land. This circumstance differed from that in which a city's settlement extended to a previously established village such as commonly happened in parts of Philadelphia, Boston, and other older eastern cities. Although there were rural villages surrounding Milwaukee which were eventually absorbed into the city itself, settlement in this period did not extend out to them. In 1880 most of the northwest side was still farm land.

Milwaukee's northwest corner in 1880 was a relatively flat area of 883 acres. Several annexations increased its size to 1996 acres by 1910 when it extended from 2.5 to 4.5 miles from the center of town. In the first decade of the new century Wards 20 and 22 comprised the city's northwest corner.[1]

The first stage in the transition from farms to urban streets and

1 Milw. Dept. of Public Works, City Engineer, MS. Maps Showing City and Ward Boundaries; MS. Annexation Map; U.S. Dept. of Interior, Geological Survey, 1958. The center of the city is defined as the confluence of the Milwaukee and Menomonee Rivers.

dwellings was a change in organization of the land through formal subdivision into city blocks and house lots. Filing a subdivision plat with the county, however, did not necessarily mean an immediate change in land use. Farming or related semirural use—such as vegetable and flower gardening, dairy and chicken farming—continued for a time. We do not know when farm operations ceased although the change in ownership, which subdivision usually implied, was probably the time when agricultural land use ended, perhaps to be replaced for a few years by no productive use while the owners awaited a rise in value.

The subdivision of Wards 20 and 22 followed a clear pattern. Subdividers first laid out tracts along neat thoroughfares, particularly the radial streets, and then parceled out the remaining land starting with the tracts closest to the center. Most of the subdivision occurred in the mid-1880's before the streetcar had pushed out that far. The mean year of subdivision for the sample blocks was 1886. After 1893 only the extreme northwest portion of the area remained to be subdivided.

In laying out Wards 20 and 22 the subdividers extended the existing gridiron pattern of the city's streets. Only three radial streets crossed the area and all of them, Fond du Lac Avenue, Hopkins Avenue, and Teutonia Avenue, had been country roads long before subdivision. The area lacked any spatial focus whatsoever, and the city failed to reserve any significant space for public use. There was a large Protestant cemetery partly extending into Ward 20. A Milwaukee Road track ran northward from the Menomonee Valley directly through the western segment of the area. Most of the blocks and lots along the railroad tracks took no special account of it, although a few small factories did locate along the tracks in the 1890's and early twentieth century (see fig. 12).

The subdividers, in extending the gridiron arrangement, laid out very long narrow blocks. The east-west streets running through the wards were almost 700 feet apart, and the average distance between the north-south streets was 300 feet; consequently the house lots were also distressingly long and narrow. The majority of all lots in the wards measured 30 feet wide by 120 feet deep, or 3,600 square feet. Only a small portion of the lots deviated from those dimensions, and thus the average lot size was 3,740 square feet.[2]

The earliest residents of Milwaukee's northwest wards clustered around the main commercial arteries—Fond du Lac Avenue, North Avenue, and Teutonia Avenue. Only nineteen families lived on all the

2 C.N. Caspar Co., 1907; C. N. Caspar Co., 1914. This compares with an average lot size in Chicago during the same period of 3,125 sq. ft., Hoyt, 1933: p. 429.

sample blocks in 1880, and all but one were of German birth, reflecting the overwhelming predominance of German-Americans on Milwaukee's entire west side. Almost three-quarters of the family heads in the 1880 sample were unskilled laborers; an additional 16 per cent were skilled or semi-skilled workers. The heads-of-household in the 1880 sample included no professionals, major proprietors, managers, clerks, or salesmen. Although these early settlers were unskilled laborers, it would be a mistake to conclude that this was an emerging lower-income neighborhood. Rather, these families were the fringe of a large and expanding German-American community dominated by artisans and petty proprietors, and it was for that element of the population that builders provided new houses in the subsequent quarter-century.[3]

Builders took up peripheral lands for construction in the same order followed by the subdividers. Blocks along and adjacent to the main thoroughfares were improved first. The earliest structures were often stores, usually with an apartment above. Thus blocks facing and near North Avenue, Fond du Lac Avenue, Center Street, Burleigh Street, Hopkins Avenue, and Teutonia Avenue showed the earliest activity. Remaining vacant lots along the commercial streets filled later as the surrounding population grew.

The development of land for strictly residential purposes was a function of the distance of the block from the center of the city. Although there was some deviation from this pattern when owners delayed in improving their property, either for resale at higher prices or to acquire the funds for their own development, building activity on most of the land in the northwest regularly followed this order. The correlation coefficient for the relationship between the average year of construction and the distance from the center of the city for the blocks in the sample was +0.71.[4]

---

3 Analysis is based on all families living on the sample blocks in 1880; U.S. Bureau of the Census, 1880. Conzen, 1976: pp. 155, 227.

4 A correlation coefficient is a measure of association between two variables, in this case mean year of construction and distance. We must assume that the relationship between the variables is linear, that is, for each increase in distance there is an increase in year of construction. To evaluate the strength of the linear relationship we can estimate a line (usually called a regression line) which would represent the case of a perfect linear relationship, and then measure the distance of our observations (in this case facing street blocks) from the line. The correlation coefficient is actually the ratio of the total squared distances of each observation which is accounted for by using the estimated regression line. If all the points fell directly on the line the relationship was a perfect one and the coefficient 1.0 (a coefficient of –1.0 would indicate a perfect inverse relationship). The closer the coefficient is to ± 0 the stronger is the linear

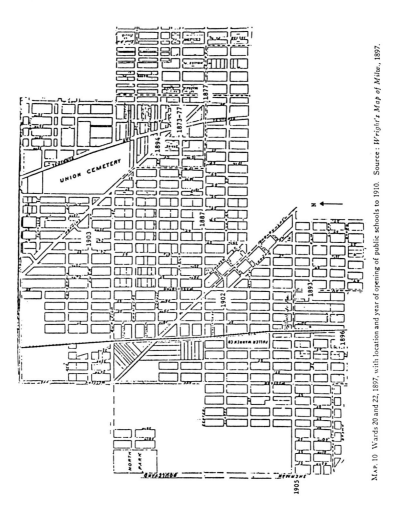

MAP. 10 Wards 20 and 22, 1897, with location and year of opening of public schools to 1910. Source: *Wright's Map of Milw.*, 1897.

association between the two variables. A coefficient at or approaching 0.0 indicates that there is no linear relationship (but not necessarily the absence of some other kind of relationship). For an introduction to this measure see Dollar and Jensen, 1971:ch. 3 or Freeman, 1965: ch. 9.

Fig. 12. Sketch of the Fuller-Warren stove factory at Milwaukee Road tracks, from Meinecke to Clarke Streets, 1892. Source: Milw. Real Estate Board, 1892.

TABLE 10

TIME-LAG BETWEEN SUBDIVISION AND CONSTRUCTION ON SAMPLE BLOCKS, WARDS 20 AND 22

Years of subdivision[a]	Number of blocks[b]	Average difference between subdivision and mean year of construction of each block in group, in years	Mean year of construction of all structures on each block in group
1857–1879[c]	9	35.4	1907
1880–1886	14	19.9	1904
1887–1893	30	15.2	1906
1894 and after	5	9.4	1909

[a] Because this analysis is based on facing street blocks rather than square blocks, the property on either side of the street was not always subdivided in the same year. In such cases I have used the mean year of subdivision for the block.

[b] Eleven blocks in the sample are excluded from this analysis because less than 60 per cent of their building permits were extant.

[c] Five of these blocks included various commercial establishments in 1905. Source: C. N. Caspar Co., 1907; 1914; sample data.

TABLE 11

PERCENTAGE OF DWELLING UNITS IN WARDS 20 AND 22 BUILT
BETWEEN 1888 AND 1905 BY SIZE AND YEAR OF CONSTRUCTION

Years of construc- tion	Average square feet per person of occupants in 1905						
	1–99	100– 199	200– 299	300– 399	400– 599	600 and over	N
1888–1893	10.3	39.4	22.6	14.2	7.7	5.8	155
1894–1899	5.2	23.7	23.0	14.8	16.3	17.0	135
1900–1905	0	10.6	28.5	22.8	24.4	13.8	123
							413

Source: Sample data.

TABLE 12

PERCENTAGE OF DWELLINGS IN WARDS 20 AND 22 BY YEAR
OF CONSTRUCTION AND NUMBER OF DWELLING UNITS

Years of Construction[b]	Number of Dwelling Units[a]			
	One Family	Two Families	Three Families	N
Before 1888	80.2	18.7	1.1	91
Sometime between 1888–1905	82.5	17.7		164
1888–1893	83.2	13.4	3.4	149
1894–1899	80.4	19.6		138
1900–1905	76.7	23.4		146
After 1905	48.8	51.2		346

[a] For all dwelling built up to 1905 the number of families is based upon number of families occupying the dwelling at the time of the 1905 census. After 1905, data are based upon descriptions on building permits.
[b] Milwaukee first required permits in 1888. The assessment records were checked for 1888 to determine buildings standing in that year. Assessment records were also checked in 1905. The 164 dwellings in the second category had no extant permits, but the assessment rolls showed no dwelling in 1888 and one in 1905.
Source: Sample data.

6 Sample data.

The first construction activity on most blocks occurred within five
to ten years of subdivision, but there was considerable variation between
the date of subdivision and the mean year of construction of the dwellings on a given block. For blocks subdivided before 1880 an average of
thirty-five years elapsed between the subdivision and the mean year of
dwelling construction. That considerable time lag narrowed for blocks
subdivided after 1880 (see table 10). The subdividers' practice of first
platting lots on likely transit arteries accounts for part of the lag.

Subdivision and new construction activity in Milwaukee, as in
other American cities, occurred in speculative cycles. Rapid population
growth and favorable business conditions provided considerable stimul-
ation for increases in subdivision and construction activities, which
reached a peak when available house lots and homes exceeded the
immediate needs of the population. The lots subdivided in one cycle
often lay undeveloped until the next. Milwaukee grew by 37 percent in
the first half of the 1880's, which helped stimulate a rising speculative
cycle in lots and houses similar to that experienced by other cities at that
time.[5] This also accounts for the lag between subdivision and construction.

Between the late 1880's and the early twentieth century the trend
in new construction was towards larger structures, and, after 1900,
towards two-family dwellings. Comparing dwellings standing in 1905
by square feet per person, with the year of construction, reveals the trend
to larger units (table 11). The increase in the proportion of all dwellings
built for two families was slight until after 1900, and it was not until after
1905 that the two-family home came to dominate the construction
activity. For all dwellings built between 1888 and 1905 the average gross
square feet per dwelling was 1,594.1.[6]

The four operations in the conversion of open field to urban land
suggested at the outset of this chapter—subdivision, housing, services,
population—were all necessary to complete the suburban environment,
but they did not necessarily occur in a rigid sequence. The installation
of urban services was the most variable of the four elements. Five services are evaluated: the arrival of nearby streetcar service, the construction of new public elementary schools, water mains, sewer lines, and
graded streets. The timing of the arrival of these services is indicative
of the level of services that a particular population could support and of

---

5 Hoyt, 1933, provides a comprehensive treatment of factors affecting land values,
sales, and speculative cycles, see esp.: ch. 7; Ward, 1971: p. 129.

6 Sample data.

FIG. 13. 2835 and 2839 N. 23rd Street. Originally identical cottages built in 1891. Dimensions: 20 X 30 ft. Part of a group of twenty-seven cottages built by A. K. Mayhew, a real estate speculator and manufacturer. Typical of the small one-family homes of the period. Picture, 1974.

FIG. 14. 2519, 2525, and 2527 N. 28th Street. Three typical cottages built in 1893, 1899, and 1895; dimensions: 20 X 42, 24 X 42, 20 X 44 ft.; cost: $750, $1,250, $800. Picture, 1974.

FIG. 15. East side of 2200 block, N. 34th Street. Typical block of large one- and two-family dwellings. Built, from left to right, 1906, 1902, 1902, unknown, 1922. Picture, 1974.

FIG. 16. 1815-17 W. Clarke Street. Typical large two-family flat, built in 1907 at a cost of $5,000. Dimensions: 28 x 44 ft. Picture, 1994.

the quality of the urban environment at a given time. To measure the degree of development required for streetcars, water mains, sewer lines, and graded streets we can employ the concept of a threshold population. The threshold population is the percentage of the building lots on a block that contained a structure when the city or the streetcar companies acted to provide new services.[7] The threshold population measure does not imply that the decision-makers had some particular and automatic figure in mind for planning the new services which has since become lost to posterity. Rather, it is offered as a measure of the level of development necessary to support those services, as well as to discover whether any pattern existed in the sequence of providing those services.[8] The schools are evaluated somewhat differently since we cannot tie that service to particular blocks.

A sequence of development is clear: houses and people came first, although before very many had arrived, convenient streetcar service followed. This stage in the process is already well known for cities generally and requires no extensive elaboration here. Urban land is of little value for residential purposes if it is inaccessible in economic terms to the

TABLE 13

MEAN THRESHOLD POPULATION PERCENTAGES FOR
EACH SERVICE BY DATE OF INSTALLATION,
WARDS 20 AND 22, SAMPLE BLOCKS

	Services			
	Streetcar	Water Main	Sewer Main	Improved Street
Date of Installation				
Before 1888	5.7	—	—	14.3
1888–1889	13.2	16.3	5.8	6.5
1890–1893	16.9	22.4	25.0	18.3
1894–1899	10.2	16.7	27.9	30.2
1900–1905	8.6	21.9	19.0	27.3
1906 and after	—	26.0	27.9	34.9
All Years	14.3	21.2	23.4	26.1

Source: See footnote 10.

7 The threshold population is based on the number of buildings standing at the end of the calendar year before the new services arrived. The city planned its improve- ments in the early spring; the degree of development at that time, therefore, would be most meaningful.

8 See the discussion above, ch. 2 and table 4.

most likely users. Wards 20 and 22 were just a little too far from the center of town for convenient walking. But to say that the streetcar was the first service is only to tell a part of the story, the most obvious part.[9]

More important, in terms of what is less well known about the process of urban expansion, is that the threshold populations for water and sewer services were only slightly higher than those for the streetcar. The average threshold population for streetcar service was 14.3 percent for Wards 20 and 22, for the installation of water mains the threshold was 21.2 percent, for sewers, 23.4 percent, and for improved streets, 26.1 percent. Before most new blocks were only one-third developed, they could provide the finished urban environment of adequate transportation, clean water, a sewer system, and a graded and roughly paved street so essential to making urban living safe and comfortable.[10]

Municipal services such as public schools, fire stations, and police precincts which were provided on a district or ward basis also affected the quality of the new urban environments. Those services cannot be evaluated by threshold populations because the necessary population data for the appropriate spatial units are not available, but we can determine the timing and location of new facilities. The most important of those services for an understanding of the city-building process were the public schools because the new neighborhoods were disproportionately devoted to childraising. Not all school-age children attended school, and not all those who attended went to public schools. In 1910, 41,633 children attended public school for thirty-two weeks of the school year and 24,182 attended private school.[11]

There was a recurrent pattern to the manner in which the city extended educational facilities into peripheral areas. The first school facilities came long before the peripheral areas constituted separate wards. Thus the first school in what later became Ward 20 opened in

---

9 Warner, 1962: pp. 21-22; Fellman, 1957: pp. 59-82. Convenient service was defined as within four blocks of any streetcar line.

10 Milw. Board of Public Works, 1881-1911; Milw. Dept. of Public Works, Office of Water Engineer, MS. Atlases of the Water System; Milw. Dept. of Public Works, Office of Sewer Engineer, MS. Atlases of the Sewer System; Milw. Dept. of Public Works, City Engineer, Card File Showing History of Street Imporvements in Milw.; Caspar and Zahn, 1886; Cf.N. Caspar Co., 1904; Silas Chapman, 1891; Silas Chapman, 1894; The Milwaukee Electric Railway and Light Co., 1909; John I. Beggs, 1898; Matthews-Northrup, 1891; Wright's *Map of Milwaukee*, 1911; Wright's *City Directory of Milwaukee*, 1880-1893.

11 Milw. Board of School Commissioners, 1910: pp. 68, 190. The decision to construct a new school, the choice of site, and the selection of the plans were made jointly by the School Commissioners and the Common Council.

1873 in rented quarters. It served just the first two grades and was replaced with a two-room frame building three years later.[12] The two- or four room frame building, just to serve primary grades, was common practice in the '80's and '90's.

The school populations of Wards 20 and 22 increased steadily and various makeshift arrangements arose to handle the load. Temporary frame classrooms on the school grounds became a common sight; some schools had five in use at various times. Classes were held in hallways and attics, and as a final resort, some schools were forced to split sessions. The Board of School Commissioners responded with new schools and additions to existing buildings, but not fast enough. Often a school addition intended to replace temporary classrooms was so inadequate when completed that the temporary classrooms remained. In 1898 the board opened a new large facility at 12th and Center Streets to replace the original frame building, but conditions were such that the frame structure had to continue in service. By 1910 there were four schools in Ward 20, plus North Division High School, and three schools in Ward 22, but three of those seven elementary schools had over 900 pupils each.[13] (Map 10 shows the location of all the schools in and near Wards 20 and 22 with the dates the schools opened. Appendix B provides additional information on the evolution of the facilities in those wards.)

FIG. 17. Elementary school at 12th and Center Streets. Second building on the site, built in 1898. Typical of the large public schools of the area. Picture, 1974.

---

12 Milw. Board of School Commissioners, 1874: p. 217.

13 Milw. Board of School Commissioners, 1898: p. 60; 1910: pp. 178-179.

Throughout the period of rapid growth, the city was constantly trying to keep up with the demand. As fast as it could open new schools and build additions, the enrollments grew. Clearly, the households with growing families were not attracted to peripheral wards because of an ample supply of classroom space; rather, it would appear that space inside and outside the home took priority over space inside the school.

Urban expansion was both a process of the physical transformation of a certain land area and of the population movement into a new housing stock. We can trace the evolution of the area's housing stock from 1888 on, although we can inspect the spatial distribution of the population at only one particular year, 1905. There is nothing special about the year 1905 to attract our attention except the enumeration of the last Wisconsin state census. It does not allow us to detect any trend in the character of the population. But precisely because 1905 was not a watershed or the end or beginning of a boom, of an era, or of a political movement, it furnishes a useful bench mark on urban expansion. It does provide some clues to the housing needs of various population groups.

Keeping in mind that in each case the house preceded the family, it is useful first to analyze the demographic character and housing needs of the population in 1905, and then examine how the public and private institutions and a "free market" in houses and land allocated that housing stock amongst the population.

Milwaukee's new neighborhoods were the sections dispropor- tionately devoted to childraising (see map 9). Thus we find that the mean family size of the northwest wards in 1905, 4.83, persons was larger than the city-wide average of 4.68 persons. The disparity would be even greater if the city-wide figure did not include the institutional popu- lation.[14]

The chief distinguishing characteristic of these families was their middle position both in social and in economic terms. Ethnically, they were neither recent immigrants nor native American stock; they were overwhelmingly German. Fifty-five percent of the family heads were German-born, and 27.8 percent more were native-born of German

---

14 Sample data; Wis. Secretary of State, 1906: p. 36. The sample data included only private families. See U.S. Bureau of the Census, 1902: 2: pp. clvii, clxiv. The institutional population included prisons, orphanages, convents, boarding houses, and boarding schools, the inhabitants of which were all considered as a single "family." The 1905 state census did not tabulate private families and institutional families separately as did the 1900 federal census. In 1900 the citywide average of all families was 4.77, and for private families it was 4.67. The 1905 average for private families, therefore, was undoubtedly lower than 4.68.

parents. They were also predominantly artisans, shopkeepers, foremen, and minor officials, which placed them roughly in the middle of the socioeconomic order.

The family's characteristics that influenced a family's housing choice and location were: stage in the family life cycle, socioeconomic class, and ethnic background. These characteristics tended to be interrelated, and an understanding of those relationships facilitates explanation of the allocation of the housing stock. The interrelationships are most easily seen if we look at families by stage in the life cycle as measured by age of the family head.

New families were, of course, smaller than the average. (Table 14 shows the mean household size of each age group.) All households whose head was below age twenty-five numbered three or less. Younger family heads were also more likely than the group as a whole to be native-born. The mean age of all United States-born sample members was 36.6, fully ten years less than the mean of German-born family heads. The reason was that most German migration had occurred in the middle decades of the nineteenth century and the native-born family heads were often children of German immigrants (see Table 15).

Younger family heads also tended to cluster in the white-collar occupational groups, such as agents and clerks, professionals, and semi-professionals. The mean ages of persons in those categories were all several years lower than the mean for the entire sample (see Tables 16 and 17).[15] These younger, native-born family heads gravitated to jobs in a rapidly expanding sector of the economy where a knowledge of language and arithmetic skills were useful or essential--positions for which native-born persons were better able to obtain the necessary formal training. Since many of the younger, native-born family-heads were sons of German immigrants, these relationships are also suggestive of an inter-generational process of social mobility.[16]

Household heads in the middle stage of the life cycle, between ages forty and sixty, tended to have the largest households. Family size increased steadily with age of the head until it reached a peak of 6.65 persons for the fifty to fifty-four year age group. On the average, household size then began to decline as grown children departed to

---

15   See Simon, 1971: pp. 182, 184-187, 189-195, 197-202 for the percentage tables showing these relationships.

16   On the concentration of second generation immigrants in white-collar occupations see Woods and Kennedy, 1969: pp. 132, 158. On the decline in the use of German see Still, 1948: p. 266; U.S. Congress, Senate, 1911: p. 257.

TABLE 14

MEAN HOUSEHOLD SIZE OF EACH AGE GROUP OF
HOUSEHOLD HEADS, WARDS 20 AND 22, 1905

Age Group of Household Head	Mean Household Size	Number
20–24	2.93	21
25–29	3.66	73
30–34	4.49	108
35–39	4.76	128
40–44	5.48	117
45–49	5.66	102
50–54	6.65	87
55–59	4.88	46
60 and over	3.25	65

Source: Sample data.

TABLE 15

CHARACTERISTICS OF SAMPLE HEADS OF HOUSEHOLD
BY PLACE OF BIRTH, WARDS 20 AND 22, 1905

Place of Birth	Number	Percentage	Mean Age of House-hold Head	Mean Household Size
United States	297	39.2	36.6	4.4
Germany	415	54.8	46.7	5.1
Britain	9	1.2	42.0	4.2
Ireland	3	0.4	63.3	6.0
All other Countries	26	3.4	44.0	5.4
Country Unknown	7	0.9	32.9	4.0
Total	757	100	42.8	4.8

Source: Sample data.

establish their own families.

There was also a tendency for the percentage of household heads of German birth to increase with age. Over two-thirds of family heads in their fifties were in that category as compared to family heads aged thirty to thirty-four, over half of whom were native-born of German parentage. Family heads of middle age tended to work with their hands. Almost a third of those in their fifties were unskilled workers, while less than a quarter were skilled, semi-skilled, or unskilled workers. The percentage of skilled artisans, the largest occupational group, was very similar for most all age groups and the mean age of those workers was close to the mean for all family heads.

Families in the late stage of the life cycle again were small in size. The vast majority of the family heads were German-born (over 85 percent). A quarter of these men and women were retired or unemployed, and the balance did not tend to cluster in any particular occupational group.

With these interrelationships among the characteristics of the families in mind, we can examine how the housing stock was allocated on the sample blocks. There are three basic measures available to analyze the housing stock: size of the dwelling unit, tenancy status, and number of families in the dwelling. The allocation of the area's dwellings by those characteristics was a function of the varying needs and resources of the population.

Tenancy status was closely associated with both the age of the family head and household size. Younger families tended to rent, but the tendency fell steadily as age increased until family heads reached age sixty, when the percentage of renters again rose slightly. Thus, three-quarters of all household heads under thirty rented, as did just over one-quarter of those in their fifties. But almost 40 percent of those in their sixties were renters. Table 18 shows the percentage of each age group in each tenancy status and the mean age and household size.

The tendency to hold a mortgage also increased with age, except that those over sixty were more likely to own free or to rent than to carry an encumbrance. Since both young and old families tended to be small, the mean size of all renting families was 4.4 persons, but of all owning families, it was over 5. Therefore, younger households, and all smaller households, gravitated towards rental units. Larger households were more likely to own because they had the time to accumulate the necessary down payment, and because ownership usually meant more space inside and outside the home.

TABLE 16

CHARACTERISTICS OF SAMPLE HEADS OF HOUSEHOLD
BY OCCUPATION, WARDS 20 AND 22, 1905

Occupational Groups	Number	Percentage	Mean Age of House- hold Head	Mean Household Size
Professionals	17	2.3	37.2	4.6
Major Proprietors	4	0.5	47.5	6.3
Semi-Professionals	4	0.5	39.5	4.0
Agents, Clerks	83	11.0	37.6	4.4
Shopkeepers	114	15.1	43.4	4.9
Skilled Workers	294	39.0	40.2	4.7
Semi-skilled Workers	76	10.1	42.6	5.4
Unskilled Workers	115	15.3	45.4	5.4
Unemployed, Retired Unknown	47	6.2	57.5	3.4
Total	754	100	42.8	4.8

Source: Sample data.

TABLE 17

PERCENTAGE OF FIRST AND SECOND GENERATION GERMAN
HEADS OF HOUSEHOLD BY OCCUPATION,
WARDS 20 AND 22, 1905

	U.S.-born of German-born Parents	German-born
Professionals	2.9	2.2
Major Proprietors	0.5	0.3
Semi-Professionals	0.5	0.5
Agents, Clerks	17.6	5.7
Shopkeepers	20.0	11.6
Skilled Workers	37.6	41.7
Semi-Skilled Workers	10.2	11.6
Unskilled Workers	8.9	22.7
Unemployed, Retired, Unknown	1.9	3.7
Number	205	405

Source: Sample data.

[15] See Simon, 1971: pp. 182, 184–187, 189–195, 197–202 for the percentage tables showing these relationships.
[16] On the concentration of second generation immigrants in white-collar occupations see Woods and Kennedy, 1969: pp. 132, 158. On the decline in the use of German see Still, 1948: p. 266; U.S. Congress, Senate, 1911: p. 257.

TABLE 18

PERCENTAGE OF EACH AGE GROUP OF SAMPLE HEADS OF
HOUSEHOLD BY TENANCY STATUS AND MEAN AGE AND
HOUSEHOLD SIZE, WARDS 20 AND 22, 1905

| | Tenancy Status | | | | |
| | Own | | | | |
Age	Free	Mortgaged	Encumbrance Unknown	Rent	N
20–29	4.4	19.6	1.1	75.0	92
30–34	6.6	30.2	—	63.2	106
35–39	13.6	32.0	2.4	52.0	125
40–44	20.9	41.7	3.0	34.8	115
45–49	25.3	43.4	1.0	30.3	99
50–59	28.8	43.1	0.1	27.3	132
60+	31.7	28.3	1.7	38.3	60
Mean age, years	48.9	43.8	39.8	38.8	
Mean Household Size	5.1	5.2	5.4	4.4	

Source: Sample data.

TABLE 19

PERCENTAGE OF SMALLEST AND LARGEST HOUSEHOLDS WITH
LESS THAN 300 SQUARE FEET AND MORE THAN 600 SQUARE
FEET PER PERSON WITHIN THE DWELLING, BY OCCUPA-
TION OF THE HEAD OF THE HOUSEHOLD, WARDS 20 and
22, 1905

| | Household Size | | | | | |
| | 1 or 2 persons | | | 7 or more persons | | |
	Per cent Under 300 Sq. Ft. per Person	Per cent Over 600 Sq. Ft. per Person	N	Per cent Under 300 Sq. Ft. per Person	Per cent Over 600 Sq. Ft. per Person	N
Professionals	0	80.0	5	75.0	0	4
Major Proprietors	—	—	0	0	50.0	2
Semi-Professionals	—	—	0	100	0	1
Agents, Clerks	12.5	62.5	8	80.0	0	10
Shopkeepers	16.7	83.3	·6	73.3	0	15
Skilled Workers	15.8	47.4	19	94.4	0	18
Semi-Skilled	0	0	2	87.5	0	8
Unskilled Workers	0	37.5	8	100.0	0	17
Unemployed, Retired, Unknown	0	50.0	4	100.0	0	1

Source: Sample data.

Although homeownership was associated with larger households and more dwelling space, it did not mean more space per person. In fact, smaller families had more space per person within the dwelling unit than larger families. The overall correlation coefficient for the relationship between household size and square feet per person was -0.60 for Ward 20 and -0.51 for Ward 22. The reason was that certain parts of the dwelling units were common areas and did not increase in the same proportion as an increase in family size. A household of eight may have had a home with a considerably larger kitchen and parlor than a family of four, but not necessarily twice as large.

In Wards 20 and 22 the ability to pay, as measured by occupation, had an appreciable effect only on space within the dwelling for persons of similar household size. Table 19 shows the percentage of small and large households having less than 300 and more than 600 square feet per person for each occupational group. Among small households, considerably higher percentages of professionals and proprietors had over 600 square feet per person than semi-skilled or unskilled workers. Among large families, all of the lower paying occupational groups had less than 300 square feet per person in the dwelling.

FIG. 18. 2724, 2728, and 2730 W. Concordia Street. Typical one-family bungalows of World War I era. Built in 1918 at a cost of $3,500-$3,800 each. Picture, 1994.

The relationships among household size and age, occupation, and dwelling space are not unfamiliar to the study of the family or housing patterns.[17] What is significant for the urban historian, however, is that such demographic aspects of urban expansion have received little attention. Historians in general and urban historians in particular have long been preoccupied with the significance of class, occupation, and wealth. Sam Warner, Zane Miller, Lloyd Rodwin, and others have explained the "suburbanization" movement of the middle and late nineteenth century almost solely in class terms.[18] Warner told us he was dealing with the upper half of Boston's population, indicating that the lower half was occupying the older housing the suburbanites left behind. To be sure, there is a powerful socioeconomic dimension to an analysis of urban expansion, but it is also clear that other factors influenced the residence and the environment of turn-of-the-century urbanites.

The physical attributes of the new urban neighborhood in Milwaukee's northwest side were a function of the resources and values of the families who settled there. Because of the particular locational advantages and amenities of the area, not all families were equally attracted. The northwest was attractive to German families who desired to remain near others of a shared cultural heritage. The area also offered access to employment opportunities for skilled artisans and petty shopkeepers willing or able to use the streetcar. Some discrimination in the sale or rental of housing may have kept down the number of East European immigrants in Wards 20 and 22, but the other wards offered them better access to employment for the unskilled combined with established social, religious, and cultural institutions.[19] At the other extreme, more affluent occupational groups, who also often enjoyed higher prestige, could locate in more attractive neighborhoods, again with other families of similar social background. Subdividers and builders responded to the outward movement of the German artisans with lots and homes reflecting the contemporary middle class standards of style and design and within the price range of the group. The streetcar lines extended their service outward as the first few homes went up in the area. The city provided a critical incentive with new schools and the

17 See Winnick, 1957: pp. 8-11.

18 Warner, 1962: pp. 46, 58, 60, 64; Miller, 1968: pp. 31- 32, 46-49; Rodwin, 1961: p. 102.

19 Evidence of discrimination on the basis of ethnic origin in the sale or rental of housing is virtually non-existent, but such discrimination most likely did occur. For a discussion of the issue see Chudacoff, 1972: p. 127.

citizens taxed themselves for water and sewers and   graded streets when
the blocks were about a quarter occupied.

Not all segments of this German middle class responded equally to
the blandishments of eager real estate promoters and streetcar lines.
Outlying homes offered more interior and exterior space and were more
attractive to those with larger families. The household size of the two
wards was larger than the city mean. The housing stock included a large
number of two-family flats to provide some investment income for the
owner and to reduce land acquisition costs. Consequently the area
included many potential rental units. Young couples, often with one
child, and some older families, whose children had departed, gravitated
to the rental units, which scattered through the wards. The smaller
families consequently had fewer gross square feet in their dwellings, but
usually more square feet per person than the average family.

To evaluate the quality of this new environment fully, we must also
compare it with the new neighborhoods arising simultaneously in other
segments of the city.

4. DOUBLING-UP AND DELAYED
SERVICES IN WARD 14

IN THE SPRING of 1905 Bartholomew Koperski and his wife and six children lived at 1805 South Twelfth Street in Milwaukee's Ward 14. Koperski was forty-six years old, Polish-born, and worked as a railroad car inspector. He owned his home without a mortgage, but he still rented out part of it, probably the basement, to George Krzyzaniak, a twenty-nine-year-old Polish-born carpenter with a wife and two children. All twelve people lived in a small, one and a half story frame cottage built in 1892. The home measured only 22 feet wide by 40 feet deep and sat close to the street on a 30 by 115 foot lot.

Around the corner front the Koperski's, at 1963 South 11th Street, was Frank Szolkowski, a thirty-two-year-old Polish-born carpenter with a wife and seven children. Szolkowski rented out part of his mortgaged home to J. Jagodzinski who headed a family of three. Jagodzinski was only twenty-five-years-old; born in Wisconsin of Polish parents, he worked as an unskilled laborer. These two families lived in a home built in 1894 with exterior dimensions of 22 by 46 feet.

Around another corner were the Banaszynski's. Julia was a sixty-year-old widow; her son Albert worked as a clerk, but also earned some extra money in 1905 by serving as an enumerator for the Wisconsin state census. They lived at 738 Burnham Street in a small home built before 1888.

Between 1885 and 1910 Ward 14 constituted the southwest corner of the city. [1] The ward's general pattern of development displayed some striking differences from that of Wards 20 and 22. Although the proportions of children and of homeowners were higher than at the northwest periphery, the homes were smaller and the general quality of the physical environment less adequate. Because of the high rate of ownership, however, the residents had a remarkable opportunity to manipulate the environment to meet their immediate needs.

Ward 14 was an 870-acre tract lying between two and three miles from the center of the city. It contained two small parks, Forest Home Cemetery, and the House of Correction. Kinnickinnic Creek meandered

---

1 Milw. Dept. of Public Works, City Engineer, MS. Maps Showing City and Ward Boundaries; MS. Annexation Map.

FIG. 19. 1805 S. 12th Street, residence of B. Koperski, 1905. Picture, 1974.

FIG. 20. 1963 S. 11th Street, residence of Frank Szolkowski, 1905. Picture, 1974.

along the southern portion of the ward.[2] Forest Home Cemetery had a considerable impact on the ward's early development. Because cemeteries were popular recreational areas in the late nineteenth century before urban parks were widespread, Forest Home attracted mass transportation earlier than would otherwise have been the case.[3] In 1877 the Cream City Street Railway Company built a line along Forest Home Avenue to the Cemetery. Although service along the route was irregular for some years, the line did make the adjacent land accessible to the rest of the City.[4]

The subdivision of Ward 14 followed a pattern quite similar to that of Wards 20 and 22. Subdividers carved up the land, systematically moving outward from areas of existing settlement. The correlation coefficient for the relationship between distance from the city center and year of subdivision of the sample blocks was +.67. The street pattern was a grid, but with even longer and narrower blocks than on the northwest side. Since most of the north-south blocks contained 38 to 44 platted lots, the long, narrow frontage lots dominated. Lots were usually 30 by 120 feet (3,600 square feet), with the mean for the sample blocks being 3,572 square feet.[5] The grid pattern precluded any real focus for the area, although the two diagonal streets, which again predated subdivision, were retained. Subdivision along those streets occurred earlier than their distance would suggest, because they were potential commercial avenues. The subdividers also ignored the ward's principal natural feature, Kinnickinnic Creek, cutting their blocks and lots right across it as though it did not exist.

The ward was subdivided between the 1870's and the 1890's with most of the activity during the real estate boom of the late '80's. The mean year of subdivision for all the sample blocks was 1885. The city annexed the southern portion of the ward in 1889, further stimulating rapid subdivision of that tract.

The cemetery and the House of Correction helped attract some inhabitants to the area in the 1870's. Land costs were relatively low because the area was still beyond the settled portion of the city.[6] At the time of the 1880 federal census there were only fifty-three households on

---

2 U.S. Dept. of Interior, Geological Survey, 1958; 1958a.

3 Reps., 1965: ch. 12.

4 McShane, 1975: pp. 53, 56, 61; Temkin, 1970: pp. 11-12.

5 C. N. Caspar Co., 1907.

6 Milw. Tax Commissioner, 1910: pp. 18-21.

FIG. 21. 738 W. Burnham Avenue, residence of Julia and Albert Banaszynski, 1905. Picture, 1994.

TABLE 20

PROFILE OF HEADS OF HOUSEHOLDS ON
WARD 14 SAMPLE BLOCKS, 1880

Occupations	Number	Per cent	Place of Birth	Number	Per cent
Shopkeepers	2	4	United States	1	2
Skilled workers	3	6	Bohemia	1	2
Semi-skilled workers	1	2	Germany	51	96
Unskilled workers	46	87		—	—
Retired, Unemployed,			Total	53	100
Unknown	1	2			
	—	—	Mean Age:	38.5	
Total	53	100			
			Mean Family Size:		4.5

Source: Sample data.

all the sample blocks.[7] Almost 90 percent of these household heads were unskilled laborers. Over 95 percent were German born, although some may have, in fact, been born in German controlled Poland (see table 20). This distribution is strikingly similar to that found in Wards 20-22 in 1880. It suggests that lands at the fringe, lacking services or good access, continued to attract low-income families. Since the city was so heavily German in 1880, it is not surprising to find them in Ward 14. However, the large Polish influx to the south side in the 1880's and '90's overwhelmed other ethnic groups in the area. In the late years of the century the anticipated market for new homes in Ward 14 were Polish immigrant families.

In the twenty-five years after 1880, subdividers, builders, speculators, homeowners, and tenants transformed Ward 14 from an outlying, lightly settled periphery of open spaces into a dense and complex urban neighborhood. The sample blocks that held 53 households in 1880 held 457 in 1905. The ward as a whole became the most populous in the city. Although the resultant environment was distinct in many ways from that on the northwest side, several aspects of the building process operated in essentially the same manner.

Three factors affected the timing of a particular block's development: distance from the city center, year of subdivision, and any anticipated exceptional value of the site. The correlation coefficient between distance from the city center and mean year of construction was +.60. In other words, builders tended to move outward in a reasonably systematic manner. However, because of rapid population pressure, there was a decline over time in the average number of years a subdivided parcel remained undeveloped. Subdivision on the sample blocks all occurred in three periods, 1872-1874, 1884-1889, and 1891-1896. The average time gap between subdivision and the mean year of construction of dwellings on those blocks was, respectively, 29.3, 17.7, and 15.7 years. (See tables 21 and 22.)

Blocks with an anticipated high value deviated from the general trend. Blocks along or close to the business streets, Forest Home, Windlake, and Lincoln Avenues, and South 6th Street, were developed early with considerable storefront property. But property owners with residential lots having a favorable amenity value delayed improving their land to allow for a maximum possible sale price.

The housing stock of Ward 14 was substantially different from that of Wards 20 or 22. The houses were smaller, occasionally only 20 by 30

7 U.S. Bureau of the Census, 1880.

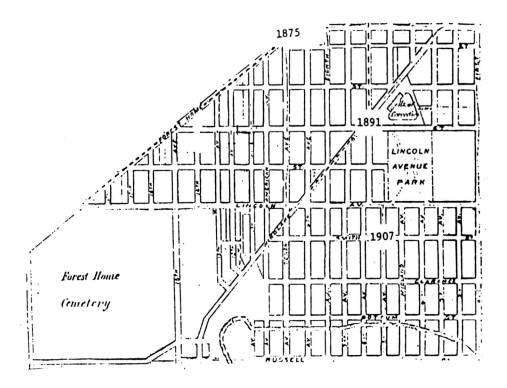

MAP 11. Ward 14, 1897, with location and year of opening of public schools to 1910.
Source: *Wright's Map of Milw.*, 1897.

TABLE 21

PERCENTAGE OF HOUSES OF EACH TYPE BY YEAR OF CONSTRUCTION, WARD 14

Year of Construction	Frame Dwellings[a]				Brick Dwellings and Stores	N
	One Family	Two Family	Three or More Families	Unspecified		
Before 1888	56.3	23.8	8.7	11.1	0	126
Before 1905[b]	60.8	35.0	4.1	0	0	97
1888–1893	58.5	39.0	5.0	2.5	0	43
1894–1899	75.0	16.7	8.3	0	0	12
1900–1905	62.5	31.3	3.1	1.6	0	64
1906–1910	49.0	31.0	2.1	10.2	0	36
1911 and after	43.3	34.3	3.0	0	10.5	67

[a] Based upon number of occupants in 1905 if known, otherwise based upon information provided by building permits. This does not clearly indicate, therefore, the extent to which houses built for one family were occupied by two or more.

[b] No permits were extant for these houses. For 44 of them the tax records show no dwelling standing in 1888. For the other 53 the tax records were not usable.

Source: Sample data.

TABLE 22

PERCENTAGE OF DWELLINGS CONSTRUCTED IN WARD 14
BETWEEN 1888–1905 BY TIME PERIOD AND AVERAGE
SQUARE FEET PER PERSON

Square Feet per Person in Dwelling, 1905	Year of Construction		
	1888–1893	1894–1899	1900–1905
1–49	10.0	9.1	6.5
50–99	44.0	36.4	35.1
100–149	14.0	18.2	19.5
150–199	18.0	9.1	11.7
200–249	8.0	0	10.4
250–299	2.0	0	2.6
300–349	2.0	9.1	1.3
350–399	0	9.1	2.6
400–599	2.0	0	5.2
600–799	0	9.1	5.2
N	50	22	77	N = 149

Source: Sample data.

FIG. 22. 913 W. Maple Street. This small cottage is typical of many of the original homes in Ward 14. The house was moved from another site to this location in 1892. Picture, 1974.

feet in exterior dimensions. The mean gross square footage for dwellings built on the sample blocks from 1888 to 1905 was 1,053.8, one-
third lower than the mean for Wards 20-22. The houses were also
plainer, lacking porches, fancy trim, or finished basements. On the
whole, the housing stock was remarkably uniform and showed little
spatial variation.

The modest homes of Ward 14 were built in anticipation of the
most likely new residents. The south side from the earliest days was the
least attractive sector of the city, and hence the least expensive. In the
1870's when the city turned towards heavy industry, and the Menomonee Valley improvements were carried out, the south side was more
accessible to a large number of jobs for unskilled labor. In those same
years the city saw its first large influx of Polish immigrants who quickly
concentrated on the inexpensive but accessible south side periphery. By
1905, the area was almost exclusively Polish; in Ward 14 three-quarters
of the household heads were Polish-born, and an additional 10 percent
were American-born of Polish parents. Germans constituted the second
largest ethnic group, 13 percent of the total. The household heads also
clustered in the lower end of the socioeconomic scale. Over half were
employed as unskilled laborers; less than 10 percent were shopkeepers,
proprietors, or white-collar workers of any sort.

In order to afford the modest new homes of Ward 14, particularly
for those seeking to purchase their own homes, many families doubled-
up in a one-family dwelling to share the costs. It was common practice
for the new homeowner, with a heavy mortgage, to rent out part of his
dwelling to another family to meet his house payments. When the mort-
gagee retired his debt he usually, but not always, took over the entire
dwelling. Sometimes he raised the home and finished the basement to
enjoy a permanent second income. One contemporary observer described the process:

. . . the custom is to erect first a four-roomed frame dwelling. When this has
been paid for, it is raised on posts to allow a semi-basement dwelling to be
constructed underneath, the lower portion being banked round with clay to
afford protection against the snow in winter. This basement or the upstairs flat
is then let by the owner, who, as soon as his funds permit, substitutes brick walls
for the timber of the basement, but the ambition of a Polish houseowner is not
crowned until he is able to have cement walks and iron railings in front of his
house. In the. . . [southwest side of the city] a very large number of these semi-
basements of wood can be seen, and although the outer aspect of the dwellings
is not unpleasing, they are in general undeniably unsanitary, being damp, as the

floor of the basement rests on the ground.[8]

The figures below show the two-level homes typical of Ward 14. They illustrate the remodeling and improvement which has been characteristic of the Polish cottages in the ward. It is evident, by visual inspection and by the building permits, that many of the original homes were raised and a finished basement added.

The quality of an urban environment was a function of the adequacy of the housing stock plus the availability of and quality of educational, transit, and sanitary services. In services, as in housing, Ward 14 showed great disparities from the northwest side.

The expansion of streetcar lines and municipal services into Ward 14 followed a different sequence from that of the northwest. Streetcars did come first, but graded streets came next, and then sewer and water mains. This was a peculiar order, because such streets had to be torn up for the mains and then regraded and graveled. The city engineer preferred to put in the sewers and water before finishing the streets, but the decision was not his alone.

FIG. 23. 1965-67 S. 11th Street, originally one story. Built in 1898 for $800. Dimensions: 22 x 48 ft. Picture, 1974.

---

8 U.S. Congress, Senate, 1911: p. 266.

FIG. 24. 2419 and 2415 S. 8th Street. 2415 built as a one-story cottage in 1891 for $700; measured 22 x 32 ft. 2419 built as a one-story cottage in 1892 for $850; measured 22 X 46 ft. In 1897 it was raised and a one-story addition built underneath. In 1911 the roof was raised and an addition added. Picture, 1974.

Generally blocks received services as they were developed and, as would be expected, in order of their distance from the city center. Commercial blocks received services relatively early. Using real estate valuation as an index of commercial activity, a strongly inverse relationship existed between the 1905 real estate valuation and the installation date of each service. (See table 23.)

Of vastly greater significance than the sequence of installation was the discrepancy between the north and south sides in the threshold populations for services. The threshold for streetcars was low, 10 percent, because of the attraction of the cemetery. But the thresholds for water, sewers, and graded streets were almost 50 percent. In other words, almost twice as many dwellings were in place on the average block in Ward 14 before those services existed than was the case in Wards 20 and 22.

To what extent did the ward's residents choose to delay the installation of the municipal services? Chapter 2 indicates that the property owners were responsible for initiating sewers, water mains, and graded streets, and, when they did not want those services, were capable of delaying them. Most of the household heads in Ward 14 were property owners and were clearly eager to keep down their housing expenses.

TABLE 23

INSTALLATION OF URBAN SERVICES ON SAMPLE BLOCKS, WARD 14

		Services		
	Streetcar	Improved Streets	Water Mains	Sewer Mains
Mean Year of Installation	1887.9	1894.9	1901.6	1900.6
Mean Threshold Percentage	10.0	45.9	46.6	47.4
Correlation Coefficients				
Distance and date	+0.47	+0.70	+0.59	+0.42
Date and real estate assessment, 1905	−0.69	−0.62	−0.39	−0.58

Source: See footnote 10, Chapter 3; sample data.

High thresholds for city services and extensive doubling-up were part of the same process. The object was the striving towards financial security and social standing by owning a home despite the major obstacles of low pay and irregular work. The thresholds and the doubling-up represented in a fundamental sense, an environmental self-determination that permitted the immigrants to struggle towards both a physical and social "zone of emergence."[9] The very real social cost of this struggle was an inferior level of public health. Ward 14, as previously indicated, had the highest crude mortality rate in the city (see table 5).

The development of three sample blocks that faced open spaces showed a significant deviation from the general trend, and thereby highlighted the factors which delayed services elsewhere in the ward. The blocks faced either one of the small parks or the cemetery. Property owners kept their lots vacant while other land was built up to allow for the maximum increase in value. The size of the lots did not deviate from the average, indicating that it was not the original subdividers, but later developers and speculators, who sought to maximize the superior site location. The provision of services to those blocks supports this contention, and also suggests the extent to which property owners themselves could influence the decisions on services. In all cases but one the three blocks received all their services before they had any inhabitants. The several owners were willing to lay out the cost of improving empty blocks to make their lots more attractive to potential buyers and residents. Surely, the investors expected to recover their additional expenses, plus interest and added profit. Table 24 compares the open-space blocks with the whole sample.[10]

In the first decade of the twentieth century, Ward 14 had the largest number of school-age children of any ward in Milwaukee. But the percentage of its children attending school was low, 40.9, compared to a city average of 56.8, and most of those children went to parochial school. In 1910, 1,194 children in Ward 14 attended public school and 4,588 attended private school. Consequently the ward only had two public elementary schools and they arrived late compared to the advent

9 Woods and Kennedy, 1969: pp. 1-42; see particularly Warner's Preface for a discussion of the concept of a zone of emergence. The term "environmental self-determination" comes from Lampard, 1973: p. 210. Warner, 1972: p. 208, refers to the new communities of the era as "a machine for social mobility."

10 There is no comparable discussion of open-space blocks in chapter 3 because there were fewer open spaces on the northwest side and only one such block appeared in the sample; it was not developed before 1905.

TABLE 24

COMPARISON OF SAMPLE BLOCKS FACING OPEN SPACES WITH
ALL SAMPLE BLOCKS, WARD 14

	Mean for All Sample Blocks	Sample Blocks Facing Open Spaces		
		I[a]	II[b]	III[c]
Year subdivided	1885	—	1891	1888
Distance from City Center, in miles	2.48	2.26	2.83	2.97
Mean Year of Construction, all dwellings	1905	1908	1907	1907
Service Thresholds:				
Streetcar	10.0	0	0	0
Water Mains	46.6	0	0	0
Sewer Mains	47.4	0	71	0
Improved Streets	45.9	0	0	0
Real Estate Assessment Valuation, 1905	$380	$580	$330	$390
Mean Lot Size, square feet	3,572	4,000	3,600	2,900

[a] South 10th Street (formerly 5th Avenue) from Beecher to Grant. This block was never formally subdivided; it faces Kosciuszko (formerly Lincoln) Park.

[b] Windlake Avenue from South 17th Street (formerly 12th Avenue) to South 18th Street (formerly 13th Avenue). It faces Pulaski Park.

[c] Lincoln Avenue from South 20th Street (formerly 15th Avenue) to South 21st Street (formerly 16th Avenue). It faces Forest Home Cemetery.

Sources: Sample data; C. N. Caspar Co., 1907; see footnote 10, Chapter 3 for sources of threshold data.

new schools on the northwest side.[11]

The traditional school organization called for opening an elementary school with all eight grades when the city created a new ward. But when Ward 14 was created in 1885, students seeking a public education still had to use the Ward 11 school on Forest Home Avenue.[12] In his annual report the superintendent of schools expressed concern over the lack of a public school in the ward. He argued that school-aged

11 Milw. Board of School Commissioners, 1910: p. 68.

12 Milw. Board of School Commissioners, 1887: p. 15; 1888: p. 17.

FIG.   25. 2100 block of S. 10th Street, facing Kosciuszko Park. Four homes in center, right to left : 2147, built: 1904, cost: $4,000, dimensions: 24 x 50 ft., families: 2; 2151, built: 1904, cost: $2,200,dimensions: 22 x 46 ft., families: 1; 2155, built: 1906,cost:$2,000, dimensions: 24 X 44 ft., families: 1; 2157, built:1907, cost: $5,500, dimensions: 25 x 66 ft., families: 2. Picture, 1974.

FIG. 26. 1738, 1734, 1730, 1726, 1722 S. Windlake Avenue. All erected by Herman Lindermann, a real estate promoter, in 1903, for $900 each; dimensions, 22 x 34 ft. Picture, 1994.

children who might have been in school if there was one nearby were roaming the streets and looking for work.

He also asserted:

> Some persons are of the opinion that the class of people living in the Fourteenth Ward do not desire school privileges, but I am assured by citizens who are in a position to know, that such statements quite misrepresent public sentiment, and that among our Polish citizens there are large numbers who would be glad to send their children to the public schools provided schools were open at a convenient distance from their homes.... [13]

In 1890 the city opened its first school in the ward, but it only served the first five grades. Older children still went to the Forest Home Avenue school. By 1900 the new school was expanded to serve all eight grades, but it was overcrowded with classes in halls and temporary rooms. In the next few years some of the grades were on split sessions. Another primary school opened in the ward in 1907 to relieve the pressure.[14] (See map 11 and Appendix B for more details on the individual schools.)

The presence of only two schools in the ward is not necessarily an indication of inferior facilities because the ward was not large in area. The main elementary school did have an enrollment of 1,225 making it the largest public elementary school in the city, but the largest school in Ward 22 was close behind with 1,130.[15] Overcrowded schools were not restricted to any one portion of the city or social class.

The provision of services to Ward 14 revealed some striking differences from Wards 20-22. Although horse cars opened the area to settlement at an early date, water mains and sewer pipes arrived late because the resident homeowners often delayed the installation of such services in order to fulfill their priority aspiration of retiring their mortgages. In many cases, of course, poverty alone caused overcrowding and toleration of unsanitary conditions. But the fact remains that numerous families did manage to save from their meager incomes and retire their mortgages. It remains to separate the owners from the renters, the crowded from the uncrowded, to complete our picture of the city-building process in Ward 14.

---

13 Milw. Board of School Commissioners, 1888: p. 42-43.

14 Milw. Board of School Commissioners, 1891: pp. 16, 46; 1900: p. 48; 1907: p. 13.

15 Milw. Board of School Commissioners, 1910: p. 68.

TABLE 25

CHARACTERISTICS OF SAMPLE HEADS OF HOUSEHOLD
BY OCCUPATION, WARD 14, 1905

Occupational Group	Number	Percentage	Mean Age Household Head	Mean Household Size
Major Proprietors	1	0.2	35.0	10.0
Agents, Clerks	11	2.4	37.7	4.9
Shopkeepers	29	6.4	41.7	6.9
Skilled Workers	127	27.9	36.8	5.1
Semi-skilled Workers	19	4.2	39.5	4.7
Unskilled Workers	237	52.1	41.1	6.0
Unemployed, Retired, Unknown	31	6.8	55.3	4.0
Total	455	100	40.6	5.6

Source: Sample data.

TABLE 26

CHARACTERISTICS OF SAMPLE HEADS OF HOUSEHOLD BY
PLACE OF BIRTH, WARD 14, 1905

Place of Birth	Number	Percentage	Mean Age Household Head	Mean Household Size
United States	48	10.5	33.5	3.9
Germany, Austria	61	13.4	44.6	5.7
All Poland	344	75.3	40.8	5.9
All Other	4	0.8	47.5	3.2

Source: Sample data.

Fig. 26. 1738, 1734, 1730, 1726, 1722 S. Windlake Avenue. All erected by Herman Lindermann, a real estate promoter, in 1903, for $900; dimensions, 22 x 34 ft.

To understand the allocation of the housing we must first examine the social and demographic characteristics of the 1905 residents. The relationships between birthplace and occupation were similar to those found in Wards 20-22. Fully 60 percent of the Polish family heads were unskilled laborers, but only 37.7 percent of the Germans and 2 percent of the native-born were in that category. Conversely, half of the native-born family heads were shopkeepers or petty officials while almost a third of the German born were skilled artisans (see tables 25, 26, and 27).[16]

The overall demographic characteristics were similar to those of the family heads of the northwest side. The family heads were slightly younger on the average (40.6 years), but because of their tendency to have more children, averaged larger families (5.65 persons per household). There were clear interrelationships among age, household size, occupation, and birthplace. (See tables 25 and 26.) Agents, clerks, and skilled workers had mean ages and household sizes well below the average, as did all persons born in the United States. Because older family heads also had smaller households, unemployed and retired heads also had a mean household size well below the average. The relationship between age and size was similar to that of Wards 20-22; the correlation below age forty-eight was +0.59, and from age forty-eight it was -0.45.

The measures available to analyze the allocation of the housing stock are size of the dwelling, number of families per dwelling, and tenancy status. The allocation of the housing stock by those measures was primarily a function of stage in the life cycle, as measured by age and household size, and of socioeconomic class, as indicated by occupation.

The amount of living space available to the individuals in Ward 14 depended first of all on the size of their households. The correlation between square feet per person and size was -0.54. Even when household size is held constant, occupation does not have a great affect on the allocation of space. Table 28 shows the percentage distribution of square feet per person for each occupational group for families of five or six persons.

The variables predicting homeownership were the same as those found in the northwest side. Both younger families and all smaller households showed a greater tendency to rent. The tendency to own rose with age and size, so that those owning without a mortgage averaged sixteen years older than renters. Table 29 shows the mean age and household size of each tenancy group.

---

16 For greater detail see Simon, 1971 : pp. 232-236, 238-242, 244-247.

TABLE 27

Percentage of Each Ethnic Group of Sample Heads of Household by Occupation, Ward 14, 1905

	Polish-Born		German-born	United States-born	All Other
	German Poland	All Other Sectors			
Major Proprietors	0.3	0	0	6.3	0
Agents, Clerks	1.6	4.5	3.3	6.3	0
Shopkeepers	5.5	0	13.1	50.0	33.3
Skilled Workers	28.0	18.2	31.1	6.3	66.7
Semi-skilled Workers	2.9	0	13.1	29.2	0
Unskilled Workers	60.8	77.3	37.7	2.1	0
Unemployed, Retired, Unknown	1.0	0	1.6	0	0
N	311	22	61	48	3

N = 445

Source: Sample data.

TABLE 28

PERCENTAGE OF HEADS OF HOUSEHOLD OF HOUSEHOLDS OF FIVE
OR SIX PERSONS OF EACH OCCUPATIONAL GROUP BY SQUARE
FEET PER PERSON, WARD 14, 1905

	Square Feet per Person			
	1–99	100–199	200 or more	N
Proprietors	0	0	100	1
Agents, Clerks	0	100	0	1
Shopkeepers	0	0	100	1
Skilled Workers	50.0	33.3	16.7	12
Semi-Skilled Workers	33.3	0	66.7	3
Unskilled Workers	40.0	46.6	13.3	15

N = 33

Source: Sample data.

TABLE 29

CHARACTERISTICS OF WARD 14 SAMPLE HOUSEHOLDS
BY TENANCY STATUS, 1905

	Tenancy Status				
		Own			
	Unknown	Free	Mortgaged	Encumbrance Unknown	Rent
Number	10	65	170	5	207
Percentage	2.2	14.2	37.2	1.1	45.3
Mean Age of Household Heads	52.1	50.0	43.6	52.0	34.4
Mean Household size	3.2	5.9	6.7	6.2	4.8

Source: Sample data.

TABLE 30

PERCENTAGE OF HEADS OF HOUSEHOLD OF EACH OCCUPATIONAL GROUP BY TENANCY STATUS, WARD 14, 1905

| | Tenancy Status | | | | | |
| | Own | | | | | |
	Unknown	Free	Mortgaged	Encumbrance Unknown	Rent	N
Major Proprietors	0	0	100.0	0	0	1
Agents, Clerks	0	0	54.5	0	45.5	11
Shopkeepers	3.5	24.1	48.3	0	24.1	29
Skilled Workers	0.7	16.9	32.4	0.7	49.3	136
Semi-skilled Workers	0	15.0	25.0	0	60.0	20
Unskilled Workers	1.6	11.5	39.9	1.2	45.3	243
Retired, Unemployed, Unknown	20.0	20.0	20.0	20.0	20.0	5
						N = 445

Source: Sample data.

The relationship between occupation and tenancy status indicated that ability to pay was a factor in dwelling allocation, although a less critical one than age and household size. Unskilled workers, who tended to be older and have larger families than the average, ranked low in percentage of renters, but also ranked low in percent of owners without a mortgage as their low-skilled positions would suggest. Conversely, proprietors and managers, with similar average age, were half as likely to rent, and twice as likely to own free and clear. Skilled workers, with the lowest average age, had the highest percentage of renters, but also had a higher percentage of those owning without a mortgage than did the unskilled (table 30).

The allocation of single and multiple family dwellings among the Ward 14 households was primarily a function of household size. Larger households tended to live in single family homes. The relationship is presented in table 31 which shows that only 30.5 percent of families of less than three persons lived in single family homes, while 60.4 percent of families of seven or more had a dwelling to themselves. This relationship was also partly a function of the tendency of older, larger families to own a home and of younger and smaller families to rent. Rental units can be single homes, but mainly occur in multi-family structures. Occupational group also affected the extent to which families shared a dwelling. Over two-thirds of all proprietors, construction workers, and white-collar workers lived in one-family dwellings, but less than 40 percent of other artisans and unskilled workers lived in such units.

The housing stock of Ward 14 was not characterized by spatial differentiation. There was some tendency for newer houses to be larger, as table 22 indicates, but the trend was not great enough to produce any marked spatial differentiation within the ward. The homogeneity of the housing accounts for the overall spatial uniformity; the occupational and ethnic homogeneity of the ward's actual and anticipated population accounts for the homogeneity of the housing stock.

Such diversity as there was within the housing stock can be traced to several identifiable factors. We can turn once again to the blocks facing open spaces to evaluate the effect of that locational advantage. Only two of the three blocks facing open space were occupied in 1905, but on both the family heads were younger and the families smaller. Both blocks had more Germans than the average and fewer unskilled workers. Table 32 compares these blocks with the averages for all those in the sample. The amenities of a desirable view and extant sewer and water services on a graded street attracted families in higher socioeconomic groups.

TABLE 31

PERCENTAGE OF HOUSEHOLDS OF EACH SIZE BY TOTAL NUMBER
OF HOUSEHOLDS LIVING IN DWELLING, WARD 14, 1905

Size of Family	Total Number of Families Living in Dwelling			
	1	2	3	N
1–2	30.5	54.2	15.3	59
3–4	29.6	60.2	10.2	98
5–6	43.2	48.0	8.1	111
7 or more	60.4	33.7	5.9	169
				N = 437

Source: Sample data.

TABLE 32

SAMPLE BLOCKS FACING OPEN SPACES COMPARED TO
WARD SAMPLE, WARD 14, 1905

	All Blocks in Sample	Sample Blocks[a]	
		I	II
Mean Age, Head	40.6	37.2	40.9
Mean Household Size	5.6	4.8	5.0
Per Cent of Household Heads			
Native-born	10.5	17.0	0
German-born	13.4	33.0	25.0
Polish-born	75.3	50.0	75.0
Unskilled	52.1	25.0	38.0
Renting	45.3	42.0	25.0
Mean Square Feet per Person	156.3	360.5	166.0

[a] See table 24 for location of blocks.
Source: Sample data.

The major determinants of the city-building process in Milwaukee's Ward 14 were distance from the center of the city and the socioeconomic status of the anticipated and actual inhabitants. Except on business thoroughfares, subdividers and builders followed an orderly outward progression in their work. Neither group showed any particular imagination or took any special risks; the limited income of the nearby residents precluded it. Builders only made extra investment in their property where an exceptional amenity factor promised a higher return.

The property owners were not only a part of a dynamic city-building process, but were also struggling with their own process of social mobility. They held down their housing costs by suffering the inconvenience, and high mortality, resulting from shared dwellings and lack of pure water or proper waste disposal. This is not to suggest that the Polish immigrants were more eager to "get ahead" than were other ethnic or occupational groups. The critical fact remains, however, that the immigrant Poles were moving from a non-propertied status to that of homeowners, and the home ownership was often of a very precarious tenure.

5. LARGE LOTS AND A VIEW: WARD 18

THE MOST attractive and desirable physical amenity in Milwaukee is Lake Michigan, and the bluffs rising along the lake shore north of the business district provide the most attractive natural setting in the city. In the late nineteenth century many of the city's wealthiest citizens lived in that neighborhood.

John Kern was a partner in John B. A. Kern and Sons, proprietors of the Eagle Flour Milling Company, a major Milwaukee industrial firm. Kern was born in Wisconsin in 1860. In 1899 he built a magnificent home on Wahl Street (then called Park Avenue) facing Lake Michigan in Milwaukee's rapidly growing Ward 18 on the city's northeast side. A man of Kern's wealth and prestige undoubtedly had the pick of virtually any house lot in the city.

In selecting a site on Wahl Street he perpetuated and reinforced the tradition of the east side, north of the business district, as the location of Milwaukee's social and economic leaders. He also selected one of the most beautiful home sites in the city.[1]

A half mile to the west, in the center of Ward 18, J. Lefebvre lived with his wife at 2597 Murray Street. Lefebvre, a sixty-year-old, Canadian-born conductor, built the two-story house in 1894. It originally cost $4,000 and measured 31 x 46 feet. By 1905 he had retired any mortgage he may have had on the dwelling, but he rented rooms to two young men in their early thirties, a New Yorker and a Pennsylvanian.

Farther north, at 3320 Hackett Street, Walter Allen, the first assistant superintendent of schools, lived in a new, large home which cost at least $3,000. Allen, a New Yorker, was fifty-four years old and sufficiently prosperous to buy the home without a mortgage and afford a resident servant.

Those affluent white-collar workers and businessmen, living in spacious and attractive dwellings, were typical of the families moving northward into Ward 18. The location was ideal. The lake was nearby or in view; the Court House, the leading banks and insurance companies, City Hall, and the specialty shops were all close by on the east side of the central business district. At the turn of the century Ward 18

---

1 Conzen, 1976: p. 109 mentions the rise of John Kern and the Eagle Flour Milling Co.

FIG. 27. 2569 N. Wahl Street, residence of John Kern, 1905. Picture, 1974.

FIG. 28. View from the residence of John Kern. Picture, 1974.

Fig. 29. 2597 N. Murray Street. Residence of J. Lefebvre, 1905. Picture, 1974.

Fig. 30. 3320 N. Hackett Street. Residence of Walter Allen, 1905. Picture, 1994.

Fig. 31. Newberry Boulevard in 1906 showing landscaping on one of Ward 18's most fashionable streets. Source: Milw. Park Commissioners, 1906: p. 10.

was the most peripheral of the east-side wards. It was the same distance from the confluence of the Milwaukee and Menomonee Rivers as were Wards 20-22 and 14, but its development was distinct from those wards in several significant ways.

Despite its proximity to the business district and older fashionable neighborhoods, Ward 18 grew more slowly and over a much longer period of time than the other wards studied. The first subdivision had occurred in 1836, but the mean year of subdivision of the sample blocks was 1878. The northern portion of the ward remained farm land through at least the 1880's and much of it was undeveloped until the 1920s.[2] The overall relationship between year of subdivision and distance from the center of the city was strong, the coefficient for the sample blocks being +.78.

Subdivision in Ward 18 was also unique because the platting gave some attention to the topography. Although the basic grid design prevailed, the streets in the narrow neck between the Milwaukee River and the lake ran in a northeasterly direction and then turned north following the course of the river and the lake. The resultant diagonal streets, particularly, Farwell and Prospect Avenues, even further increased the accessibility of the upper east side to the business district (see map 12).

2 C. N. Caspar Co., 1907; 1914.

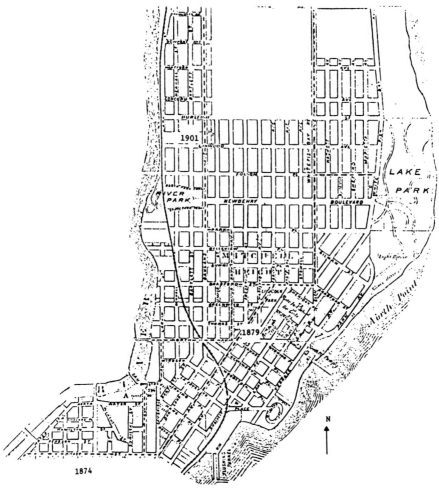

MAP 12. Ward 18, 1897, with location and year of opening of public schools to 1910.   Source: *Wright's Map of Milw.*, 1897.

Map. 12. Ward 18, 1897, with location and year of opening of public schools to 1910.
Source: Wright's Map of Milw., 1897.

Even more critical than the direction of the grid was the size of the blocks and lots. In the southern half of the ward the streets were closer together than in other wards, resulting in more nearly square blocks and lots. The lots were also larger; the mean for all sample lots in the southern half of the ward was 6,204 square feet. For the ward as a whole the mean lot size was 5,854 square feet (the mean for Ward 14 was 3,572; for Wards 20-22, 3,740).[3] One prestige subdivision in the center of the ward, Mitchell Heights, contained only eight lots on each square block. Each lot measured 90 frontage feet by 127 feet deep, or 11,430 square feet. Another exceptional subdivision plat was Newberry Boulevard Addition, north of Mitchell Heights. Its namesake street featured a landscaped boulevard running along the center of the street. The Park Commission took over and maintained the boulevard which it featured quite proudly in its 1906 *Report* (see fig. 31). The street itself was 160 feet wide, compared to the standard 60- or 70-foot streets of all the wards.[4]

The twenty-three families living on the sample blocks in 1880 all clustered around the extreme southwest portion of the ward. The most striking characteristic of those households was the low percentage of German or Polish stock and of unskilled laborers.

Household heads employed as skilled artisans or in white-collar occupations accounted for two-thirds of the families.[5] Table 33 shows the characteristics of the 1880 families. It was for precisely this segment of the population that subdividers had laid out generous blocks and lots, and it was this segment of the population which they hoped would push northward in the next quarter century.

To facilitate the northward flow of residents, the horse car network rapidly extended its routes into and through the ward. In the 1870's a horse car line extended to the southern border of the ward, although, at first, the frequency of service was poor. In the early '80's the line extended to North Avenue, probably attracted by a cluster of small

---

3 Ibid.

4 Little has been said about the width of streets because there was very slight variation-even from ward to ward. The standard street width was between 60 and 70 feet in all the wards. A few streets in Ward 18 near the lake, such as Terrace Avenue (82 feet), were exceptionally wide, but even in Mitchell Heights Subdivision the street widths were only 72 feet. In most of Ward 14 the streets were 66 feet wide.

5 U.S. Bureau of the Census, 1880. There was a small Polish community on a few blocks in the extreme southeast corner of the ward, particularly around Pulaski and Sobieski streets. None of these blocks turned up in the sample. See Reisser, 1977: *passim* for a discussion of the Poles in Ward 18.

TABLE 33

CHARACTERISTICS OF HEADS OF HOUSEHOLD ON SAMPLE BLOCKS, WARD 18, 1880

Occupational Groups	Number	Per cent	Place of Birth	Number	Per cent
Major Proprietors	2	8.7	United States	5	21.7
Agents, Clerks	2	8.7	Ireland	5	21.7
Shopkeepers	2	8.7	Germany	4	17.4
Skilled Workers	10	43.5	England	3	13.0
Unskilled Workers	5	21.7	Bohemia	3	13.0
Retired, Unemployed	2	8.7	All Other	3	13.0
Total	23	100	Total	23	100

Mean Age: 40.8   Mean Household Size: 5.0

Source: Sample data.

institutions there: a hospital, three orphanages, and the State Industrial School for Girls. In 1888 several promoters built a line northward through the entire ward and beyond to the resort community of Whitefish Bay. Service on the line was low, particularly during the winter, but it did provide some transportation through a largely unsettled portion of the city. In the early '90's the streetcar company built a crosstown line on North Avenue from Ward 18 to Fond du Lac Avenue on the west side in Ward 20. The line passed through Kilbourn Park west of the Milwaukee River, which provided the principal generator of traffic. Service on that line was also poor for some years.[6]

In 1890 the new Park Commission acquired 123.7 acres along the northern lake shore in Ward 18. The Commission invested considerable sums in landscaping, roads, a bandstand and pavilion during the next fifteen years. In the mid-'90's the streetcar company provided free summer concerts to attract customers. Except for the zoo in Washington Park on the city's far west side, the Park Commission spent more money on Lake Park than on any other in the city. In 1909 they valued it at $595,000. The park provided another pleasant amenity and attraction to builders and home buyers.[7]

Builders did not take up lots for development in Ward 18 in the systematic manner discerned in Wards 20-22 and 14. The correlation coefficient between distance from the center of the city and mean year of construction was only +.38. Thus many lots remained idle for a considerable time, some for as long as fifty years. The ten sample blocks subdivided before the Civil War showed a lag of 54.9 years between subdivision and the mean year of dwellings constructed. The gap did narrow for later subdivision. Table 34 shows the blocks grouped by time of subdivision, together with mean lag in construction, distance from the city center and the lake, and mean year of construction. The table makes clear that a large portion of the ward was built up in a relatively short span of years from the 1890's through the early twentieth century. The mean year of construction for all dwellings built after 1888 was 1908.5 with a standard deviation of 7.8 years. The standard for the mean year of subdivision was 19.7 years.

---

6 McShane, 1975: pp. 61, 112. The promoters of the Whitefish Bay line were Frederick Pabst, the brewing magnate and possibly Milwaukee's largest landowner in the period, and Guido Pfister of the large leather firm of Pfister and Vogel. On Pabst's land holdings see Cochran, 1948: p. 144.

7 Still, 1948: pp. 383-384; Milw. Park Commissioners, 1909: pp. 98-106.

TABLE 34

CHARACTERISTICS OF SAMPLE BLOCKS BY YEAR
OF SUBDIVISION

	Subdivision Periods			
	1836–1857	1867–1881	1884–1895	1899–1905
Number of Blocks	10	9	15	6
Average Gap Between Subdivision and Year of Construction	54.9	36.0	17.7	12.2
Mean Year of Construction	1904	1909	1908	1914
Distance from Center of City, in miles	2.49	2.93	3.66	3.44
Mean Distance from lake, in miles	0.40	0.30	0.74	0.80

Source: C. N. Caspar Co., 1907; 1914; sample data.

The essential distinguishing feature of the housing stock of Ward 18 was the size of the dwellings. The mean gross square feet of all homes built on the sample blocks since 1888 was 2,569.3. For homes built between 1888 and 1905 the mean was 2,229.4. For Wards 20-22 it was 1,594, and for Ward 14, 1,054. The mean square feet per person in 1905 of 570.4 compared with a mean of 156.3 in Ward 14, 363.2 in Ward 22, and 320.0 in Ward 20. Clearly, those who were responsible for building the homes in Ward 18, the small-scale developers and families buying a single lot to build their own home, met the expectations of the earlier subdividers and erected handsome and spacious dwellings, many of brick or brick veneer. The homes were often set towards the center rather than within yards of the sidewalk. There were several reasons for this. First, since the lots were often wider, the homes did not need to be as long and narrow. Second, the practice in other wards of placing houses close to the front was to permit a possible second home in the rear. Rear dwellings were found in Ward 14 and the older blocks of Ward 20. There was little expectation of rear dwellings in Ward 18. The consequence of setting the homes farther back was clear when the blocks were fully built up: even though the streets were not wider, the environment was much more spacious and open than in the south and west-side wards.[8]

8 The type of material used in construction was available from the building permits. The same information is also available from the Sanborn Insurance Maps which also indicate the location of the home on the lot. Anyone interested in obtaining a good overall impression of a city or older neighborhood, without the time and expense of a field inspection, should study a set of insurance atlases. The Library of Congress Map Division has Sanborn atlases for most American cities and a directory of the dates when each edition was published for each city. On rear houses see Reisser, 1977: pp. 133-145.

The spatial distribution of the housing stock was most affected by two overlapping factors: large lots and proximity to the lake. The nine sample blocks with the largest mean lot size (over 8,000 square feet) were all within two blocks of the lake or in the Mitchell Heights subdivision.[9] The mean gross square feet of all dwellings built on those blocks was 3,739.5. The mean square feet per person in 1905 was 862.5, as compared to the entire ward sample of 570.4. There were some changes in housing trends over time, and both time and distance from the city center did have some influence on the configuration. Those factors were secondary to the powerful attraction of the lake, however, and the large lots subdividers provided, particularly in the diagonal grid segment in the southeast corner of the ward.

There was a tendency over time towards two family dwellings, but this was not well pronounced before 1905. As in Wards 20-22, the tendency towards two-family flats, or double-deckers, greatly accelerated in the years around World War I. Some of the northern blocks of Ward 18, west of Downer Avenue, were built up with large double-deckers.[10] But two-story, single-family frame or brick veneer homes well set back on relatively large lots defined the characteristic blocks of Ward 18.

The process of providing services to the ward's homes and families was also in keeping with the activity of the subdividers and builders. The services extended outward in a reasonably systematic manner from the center of the city. It was the threshold populations that were exceptional. The vast majority of blocks in the ward acquired their services before they acquired any dwellings. The mean threshold populations for the four services were less than 5 percent. Those who could afford to purchase or rent in Ward 18 expected to move into a dwelling with running water and flush toilets, on a block with a finished street and rapid access to the rest of the city. The developers assumed the cost of installing those services and carrying the extra cost for a short period in every expectation of making the property more valuable and recouping their investment with added profit. It was the same pattern as found on blocks facing open spaces in Ward 14. Large-lot blocks and those close to the lake did not receive significantly different treatment in obtaining services because the thresholds for most blocks were zero or close to it. Table 35 shows the mean year of installation, mean threshold for each

---

9 Six of the blocks were east of Summit Ave. in the diagonal grid tract. One was across from Lake Park and two were in Mitchell Heights.

10 Simon, 1971: pp. 277, 278.

FIG. 32. 2746, 2750, 2754, 2760 N. Frederick Street. Typical block of large, one-family homes built at turn of the century. Two homes on left both built in 1900 for $4,000 each; dimensions 24 x 40 ft. Picture, 1994.

Fig. 33. 1924, 1930, and 1936-38 N. Cambridge Avenue. Typical block in southern portion of ward. House on left built before 1888. Houses on right built in 1897 and 1899. Picture, 1974.

TABLE 35

INSTALLATION OF SERVICES IN WARD 18

	Street-car	Water Mains	Sewer Pipes	Graded Streets
Mean Year of Installation	1888	1893	1893	1890
Mean Threshold Per Cent	1.9	4.0	5.1	5.0
Correlation between Installation Date and Distance from Center of City	+0.81	+0.52	+0.59	+0.67

Source: See Chapter 3, footnote 10.

FIG. 34. 2251 N. Lake Drive. Typical of large homes facing and near Lake Michigan. Built in 1890 for $7,000 with exterior dimensions of 43 X 54 ft. Picture, 1974.

service, and correlation coefficient between installation date and distance.

The pattern of adding school facilities in Ward 18 was not markedly different from the other study areas. Because of the ward's physical size, a primary school did open there in 1879 although the ward

was not actually created until 1887.[11] This school at Prospect and
Maryland Avenues became a full elementary school in 1891. Until then
students had to travel to Cass Street just below the ward boundary for
the upper grades. The Cass Street school continued to service students
in the extreme southeast corner of the ward. A branch school began in
two temporary rooms at Linwood and Bartlett Streets in 1900 while
three temporary rooms were in operation at the Maryland Avenue
school. In 1902 a twelve-room school opened at the Linwood and
Bartlett location.[12] Those two schools served 717 and 588 students
respectively during the 1909-1910 school year which was less than
either of the Ward 14 schools, but more than three of the newer schools
in Wards 20 and 22.[13] (See map 13 and Appendix B for more detail on
the individual schools.)

As suggested earlier, the socioeconomic level of most household
heads of Ward 18 was higher than those of the northwest or southwest
neighborhoods. Their movement into this peripheral area represented
an expansion of an existing concentration closer to the center of town.
The subdividers and builders thus anticipated and built for this segment of the population.

The demographic and socioeconomic indicators provided by the
1905 census sample support this pattern. Two-thirds of the sample
members were born in the United States or Britain, and a like share were
employed in some white-collar or managerial capacity. The relationships between occupation and ethnicity followed patterns similar to the
other wards. Native born family heads with native born parents concentrated in the higher paying occupations: professionals, major proprietors,
semi-professionals, and agents and clerks. Native born heads of British
or German parentage clustered more in the middle range: shopkeepers,
skilled and semi-skilled workers as well as agents and clerks. This
tendency was more pronounced among the foreign born, most of whom
were German or English (see table 36).

The correlation between age and household size was not as strong
among the Ward 18 families as in the other sample groups. The explanation lies in the large proportion of family heads native born and
employed in higher paying occupations, groups which on the whole

---

11 Milw. Board of School Commissioners, 1879: p. 12.

12 Milw. Board of School Commissioners, 1887: p. 11; 1888: p. 11; 1891: p. 48; 1900:
p. 49; 1902: p. 19.

13 Milw. Board of School Commissioners, 1910: p. 68.

TABLE 36

Per Cent of Sample Heads of Household of Each Ethnic Stock by Occupational Group, Ward 18, 1905

	United States	British Isles		Germany		All Other
		U.S.-Born	Foreign-Born	U.S.-Born	Foreign-Born	
Professionals	18.6	15.8	0	0	5.7	5.9
Major Proprietors	9.3	5.3	13.0	20.0	5.7	11.8
Semi-Professionals	7.0	0	4.4	0	0	5.9
Agents, Clerks	30.2	26.3	13.0	20.0	8.6	35.3
Shopkeepers	16.3	21.1	26.1	20.0	25.7	11.8
Skilled Workers	2.3	15.8	21.7	20.0	25.7	11.8
Semi-skilled Workers	7.0	10.5	13.0	8.0	11.4	0
Unskilled Workers	0	5.3	4.4	8.0	14.3	17.6
Retired, Unemployed, Unknown	9.3	0	4.4	4.0	2.9	0
N	43	19	23	25	35	17

N = 162

Source: Sample data.

tended to have smaller families regardless of age.[14]Native born household heads tended to be younger than the average and to have smaller
families. Among the occupational groups, only the agents, clerks, and
shopkeepers had both younger average ages and smaller families.
Professionals were older than the average, but had smaller households
while semi-professionals exhibited exactly the opposite tendencies (see
tables 37 and 38).

The allocation of the housing stock by space, location, tenancy
status, and number of families in the dwelling was primarily a function
of stage in the family life cycle and ability to pay. The correlation coefficient for the relationship between square feet per person in 1905 and
household size was .58, quite close to the correlations for the other
wards. Even holding household size constant, the ability to pay, as
suggested by occupation, does not show a strong relationship to space
within the dwelling (see table 39).

Tenancy status also showed that household size was more
influential than occupation. Table 40 shows the distribution of families
by tenancy with the mean age and size of each group. Renting households averaged four persons with forty-year-old heads, while mortgage-
holding households averaged almost five persons, and owners without
encumbrance were, on average, forty-eight-years-old. Thus, over half of
the agents and clerks (mean age, 41.5) rented, while two-thirds of the
unskilled workers (mean age, 47.3) owned with a mortgage. Unskilled
workers, however, showed considerably less incidence of ownership
without encumbrance than other groups of similar mean age. Between
a quarter and a third of the professionals and major proprietors, the next
two oldest groups, owned without encumbrance (see table 41). Finally,
the size of a household strongly affected whether it lived in a single or
multiple unit dwelling. Over four-fifths of all sample families of seven or
more lived in a single-family house, while 58 per cent of families of one
or two persons shared their living quarters.

The spatial distribution of the population was a function of the
spatial distribution of the housing stock. In Wards 20-22 and 14 the
housing stock was rather evenly distributed, but this was less true of
Ward 18. Distance from the city center, from the lake, and the location
of large-lot blocks exercised considerable influence on the distribution
of the housing stock. Further, the large-lot blocks generally coincided
with blocks close to the lake. The percentage of various groups on the

14 Compare with tables 15, 16, 25, and 26 above.

TABLE 37

CHARACTERISTICS OF SAMPLE HEADS OF HOUSEHOLD BY
OCCUPATION, WARD 18, 1905

Occupational Groups	Number	Percentage	Mean Age of House- hold Head	Mean House- hold Size
Professionals	11	6.9	45.7	3.8
Major Proprietors	18	11.3	45.2	4.4
Semi-Professionals	3	1.9	39.7	5.0
Agents, Clerks	30	18.7	41.5	3.8
Shopkeepers	32	20.0	41.8	4.2
Skilled Workers	24	15.0	40.8	5.2
Semi-skilled Workers	14	8.8	42.0	4.3
Unskilled Workers	11	6.9	47.3	5.7
Unemployed, Retired, Unknown	17	10.6	49.0	3.5
Total	160	100	43.1	4.3

Source: Sample data.

TABLE 38

CHARACTERISTICS OF SAMPLE HEADS OF HOUSEHOLD BY
PLACE OF BIRTH, WARD 18, 1905

Place of Birth	Number	Percentage	Mean Age of House- hold Head	Mean House- hold Size
United States	92	57.1	39.6	3.8
Britain	16	9.9	50.0	5.1
Ireland	8	5.0	46.9	5.6
Germany	33	20.5	46.2	5.0
All Other Countries	12	7.5	49.2	4.3
Total	161	100	43.1	4.3

Source: Sample data.

TABLE 39

PERCENTAGE OF HEADS OF HOUSEHOLD OF HOUSEHOLDS OF
THREE OR FOUR PERSONS OF EACH OCCUPATIONAL GROUP
BY SQUARE FEET PER PERSON, WARD 18, 1905

	Square Feet per Person				
	200– 399	400– 599	600– 799	800+	N
Professionals	0	75.0	0	25.0	4
Major Proprietors	14.3	14.3	42.9	28.6	7
Semi-Professionals	0	100.0	0	0	1
Agents, Clerks	9.1	72.7	18.2	0	11
Shopkeepers	16.7	50.0	25.0	8.3	12
Skilled Workers	75.0	25.0	0	0	4
Semi-Skilled Workers	14.3	57.1	28.6	0	7
Unskilled Workers	0	0	0	100.0	1

N = 47

Source: Sample data.

sample blocks can be correlated with the blocks' mean distance from the lake and the center of town to show the relationships. The correlation coefficients appear in table 42.

Proximity to the lake was desirable for the view and the access to the park. Since the lots and homes were larger than the ward average and much larger than the mean of the other study areas, the homes were undoubtedly expensive.[15] Two overlapping groups showed a moderate tendency to locate near the lake, families with older heads and those without a mortgage. Both characteristics suggest the accumulation of some wealth, because the older families had time to save, and obviously, because any mortgage had been retired. Conversely, there was a similar tendency of two other overlapping groups to locate away from the lake. The percentage of mortgage holders on a block increased with distance from the lake, as did the percentage of family heads employed as agents and clerks. One might expect the white-collar agents and clerks to be a higher status, higher income group and thus near Lake Michigan, but as indicated above, those men tended to be young, and thus to lack suf

15 Lots in Mitchell Heights, for example sold for around $45.00 per front foot, *Milw. Sentinel*, June 5, 1898.

TABLE 40

CHARACTERISTICS OF HEADS OF HOUSEHOLD BY
TENANCY STATUS, WARD 18, 1905

| | Own | | | | |
	Free	Mort-gaged	Encum-brance Unknown	Rent	Total
Number	41	39	7	65	152
Per cent	27.0	25.7	4.6	42.8	100
Mean Age of Household Head	48.2	44.6	35.0	40.0	43.1
Mean Household Size	4.4	4.9	3.4	4.0	4.3

Source: Sample data.

TABLE 41

PERCENTAGE OF HEADS OF HOUSEHOLD OF EACH OCCUPATIONAL
GROUP BY TENANCY STATUS, WARD 18, 1905

| | Tenancy Status | | | | |
| | Own | | | | |
	Free	Mort-gaged	Encum-brance Unknown	Rent	N
Professionals	33.3	16.7	8.3	41.7	12
Major Proprietors	26.7	33.3	6.7	33.3	15
Semi-Professionals	0	60.0	20.0	20.0	5
Agents, Clerks	20.6	23.5	2.9	52.9	34
Shopkeepers	33.3	13.3	3.3	50.0	30
Skilled Workers	32.0	20.0	0	48.0	25
Semi-Skilled Workers	35.7	35.7	0	28.6	14
Unskilled Workers	16.7	66.7	0	16.7	12
Retired, Unemployed, Unknown	20.0	0	40.0	40.0	5
				N = 152	

Source: Sample data.

TABLE 42

CORRELATION COEFFICIENTS BETWEEN DISTANCE FROM THE
LAKE AND FROM THE CENTER OF THE CITY, WITH SELECTED
VARIABLES OF SAMPLE BLOCKS, WARD 18, 1905

	Distance from Center of City	Distance from Lake Michigan
Mean Age of Household Heads	−.12	−.45
Mean Household Size	−.27	+.14
Percentage of Agents and Clerks	+.12	+.40
Percentage of Owners without Mortgage	+.16	−.43
Percentage of Owners with Mortgage	+.21	+.50
Percentage of Renters	−.38	−.08
Percentage of Two-Family Units	−.44	−.17

Source: Sample data.

ficient accumulated capital for larger, more expensive homes. The overlap with mortgage holders reinforces that notion.

The impact of distance from the city center was less apparent, but there was a tendency for two-family units, as of 1905, to cluster near the inner portions of the ward. Since two-family units almost invariably contained at least one rental unit, renters also tended somewhat to locate near the center of the ward, see table 43.

It is hardly surprising that family heads in higher paying and more secure occupations, and of native or British background, lived in large homes in a pleasant urban setting. The issue with regard to their services, however, had not been clearly established.[16] But beyond the simplistic notion that the rich lived better than the poor, there is much complexity and much of importance in the development of Ward 18 for understanding the city-building process. The experiences of the ward highlighted the vital and determinative role played by subdividers. They not only maximized within the limitations of the gridiron plat, the lakeside location, but they and later speculators, were prepared to withhold the land from development for some years. The process in Ward 18 also provides additional evidence to support the contention that certain segments of the central business district had a powerful

---

16 Compare Warner, 1962: pp. 31-32.

effect on residential distribution.[17] The east side was, and remains, the location of the legal, financial, and specialized retail segments of the central business district. Although the Court House moved to the west side, City Hall, the major banks, the main post office, the largest insurance company, the chamber of commerce, the prestigious hotel, and the expensive jewelry, apparel, and specialty stores remain on or near East Wisconsin Avenue. At East Wisconsin and Lake Michigan one finds the Art Museum, and next to City Hall, the Performing Arts Theatre.

Lastly, there were some basic similarities in the city-building process among Ward 18 and the other areas, despite the generally higher socioeconomic class of the residents and the greater value of the homes. Despite the larger lots, larger homes, and better services, the allocation of the housing stock within the ward remained a function of basic demographic variables—household age and size in particular—which were found elsewhere.

---

17 Compare Ward, 1971, chs. 3, 4; Conzen, 1976: ch. 5: and Hoyt, 1933: passim.

6. THE CITY-BUILDING PROCESS AND ITS IMPLICATIONS

A dynamic economy, immigration, and the formation of thousands of new households put a constant demand on Milwaukee's housing supply in the decades around the turn of the century. To meet the demand the city increased its density at the center, filled in empty lots and built rear dwellings in older wards, annexed additional territory, and created new environments along its periphery. We have concentrated on the process that created these new environments, not because they were more important, but because we cannot trace the process of neighborhood creation with the same precision before the 1880's. Moreover, these were years of considerable subdivision and building activity.[1]

Why did some families choose to settle in the peripheral wards, or, if you will, to suburbanize? For most, although not all, it meant a longer journey to work at a time when industrial workers still put in a ten- or twelve-hour day. For that very reason, peripheral land was cheap, which perhaps should have made it more desirable for the poor than the middle class and rich.[2] Such, indeed, was the classic pattern of the pre-industrial city, and was common enough in the early years of most modern cities when no transportation costs were entailed.[3] Cheaper land might mean two things: a family could occupy the same space as at an inner city location, but for less outlay, or a family could occupy more space at the same cost as before. Actually, since the residences were on larger lots than in older wards, the primary attraction was buying more space for the same dollars. While all families might be attracted by that possibility, larger families, those with growing children, most needed the extra space. The sorting out of families also revealed a greater concentration of homeowners in the peripheral wards. This is not surprising for several

1 Milw. Dept. of Building Inspector, 1964: p. 12 shows the total number of permits filed each year since 1888. Before World War I the peak in real estate sales came in 1892 at $10 million. Other peak years were 1905 and 1909. Milw. Co., County Clerk, 1881-1917.

2 There is no way to determine where the sample family heads worked. Some certainly did work near their homes. Construction workers concentrated in the northwest wards where most of the new building was located. Some in Wards 20-22 worked at the small factories emerging along the railroad tracks in that area, but most had to commute to the business district or the Menomonee Valley.

3 Sjoberg, 1960: pp. 91-103; Goheen, 1970: pp. 125-127; Conzen, 1976: ch. 5; Warner, 1962: pp. 11, 56.

reasons. First, there was a disproportion of single-family dwellings in the peripheral wards that would naturally attract the buyer. Most of the new construction was located there, which meant homes of the latest and most up-to-date standards. Furthermore, homeownership and the child-rearing stage in the life cycle largely overlapped. New families lacked sufficient time to save the large down payment required, and older families either already had their homes or rented small quarters. Older families, either because of unwillingness to take the risk, or discrimination by lending institutions, rarely held a mortgage.[4]

Previous historical explanations for suburbanization have often concentrated on the rural ideal or the search for a more satisfactory environment.[5] Nothing here contradicts those suggestions, but we have seen that some peripheral location was open to virtually all segments of the population, and that the sorting out process was indeed a selective one. Many families who disliked the congestion, the pollution, and their new immigrant neighbors must have lived in or near the business district. Many obviously weighed convenient access to employment and shopping, or proximity to friends and family, as more important than a new home and a yard.

The city-building process itself revealed fundamental differences in the quality of the environments it provided, particularly in the first generation of settlement. But there were also basic similarities that cannot be overlooked, similarities perhaps more significant for later generations than for the original residents. The environments examined here were all the products of a given time period and were all the same distance from the business and industrial center of the city. They were alike subject to the same constraints of transportation and housing technology, to similar standards of housing style and layout and arrangement on the land. Both the standards and the technology differed from those of earlier and later generations.

The city-building process began with subdivision. At that stage the similarities stood out. The grid plat and the long narrow blocks and lots were pervasive, and hence the emergent communities lacked a spatial focus. Property near Lake Michigan received favored treatment with larger lots, but virtually no deviation from the grid. The frame of reference for making those initial decisions was private profit, not a

---

4 On the structure of the mortgage market in cities during the period, see Warner, 1962: pp. 117-126; Rodwin, 1961: pp. 28-32; Chudacoff, 1972: ch. 7.

5 Warner, 1962: pp. 11-17; Rodwin, 1961: p. 94. For a more recent sympathetic view of suburbanization, see Vance, 1976:1 : p. 14.

functionally adequate environment or community need, except as such features might enhance returns. But the decisions made by hundreds of relatively obscure subdividers and developers[6] reflected public policy and a general consensus as to the appropriate layout of urban space. In 1856 the State of Wisconsin virtually wrote the grid plan into law.

The earliest residents in newly platted subdivisions preceded the streetcar, but nearby streetcar service arrived within a few years, providing incentive to both builders and buyers. Land along commercial streets, usually the ones with the streetcar lines, was developed first, and land adjacent to an amenity feature was held back. The low thresholds for streetcar service indicate its importance as a virtual prerequisite to opening peripheral land, although the city had a markedly lower than average ridership rate. It seems clear that suburbanites wanted access to the rest of the city even if they might not plan to use the streetcar for daily commutation. Certainly the immigrant working-class family struggling with a mortgage could, and probably did, afford itself of an occasional excusion to a nearby park or the zoo.[7] Thus, while the streetcar was a critical element in the city-building process by opening peripheral land for development, it exerted less of a constraining influence on family location than it did in cities where the daily ridership rates were higher.

The housing stock within each new neighborhood was homogeneous, and usually evidenced little spatial variation. The allocation of the housing stock reflected family needs for shelter and ability to pay, which in turn was a function of occupation and age of the household need. The size and quality of the housing stock among the several study areas, however, varied considerably.

Most homes built before 1910 were intended for a single family, although doubling-up was necessary for immigrant Poles to finance their mortgages, or while younger families saved their down payments. In the short run, the doubling-up was probably less desirable than the triple-deckers of some eastern cities, because it often meant basement habitations. But, even amid the doubling-up, the families did have ample yard space to utilize during part of the year, and the hope and expectation of taking over the entire dwelling at some future time. The magnitude of the hidden social and human cost of this practice is suggested by mortal-

6 For a good discussion of the kinds of men who built the new neighborhoods of Boston, see Warner, 1962: pp. 126-132.

7 The County Zoo was located in Washington Park on the north side just west of the city limits.

TABLE 43

SELECTED CHARACTERISTICS OF SAMPLE BLOCKS AND
1905 HOUSEHOLD HEADS IN STUDY AREAS

	Wards		
	20–22	14	18
Mean Distance from City Center	3.5	2.5	3.1
Mean Year of Subdivision	1886	1885	1877
Mean Lot Size, Square Feet	3,740	3,572	5,854
Mean Gross Square Feet, All Dwellings, 1888–1905	1,594	1,054	2,229
Mean Square Feet per Person	341	156	570
Mean Threshold Percentage, Water	21.2	46.6	4.0
Mean Threshold Percentage, Sewers	23.4	47.4	5.1
Mean Age, Household Head	42.8	40.6	43.1
Mean Household Size	4.8	5.6	4.3
Percentage Agents and Clerks	11.0	2.4	18.7
Percentage Skilled Workers	39.0	27.9	15.0
Percentage Unskilled Workers	15.3	52.1	8.8
Percentage German-Born	54.8	13.4	20.5
Percentage Polish-Born	—	75.3	—
Percentage Native-Born	39.2	10.5	57.1
Percentage Mortgage Holders	29.0	37.2	25.5
Percentage of Renters	42.5	45.3	42.8

Double dash indicates less than 0.10 per cent.
Source: Sample data.

ity rates. Ward 14 had the highest crude death rate in the city, although it was lower than the city-wide average of many older and larger cities.

The availability of pure water, a sewer network for waste disposal and storm drainage, and graded and paved streets are among the best available systematic measures of environmental quality. Because the property owners paid most of the installation costs and exercised considerable control over the relevant decisions, the speed of installation was a joint function of ability to pay and personal priorities. The low thresholds in Ward 18 reflected the strong financial position of the family heads. Perhaps, to use Lloyd Rodwin's phrase, it also reflected their more thorough immersion in "middle-class standards."[8]

The construction of public schools followed a different pattern from

---

8 Rodwin, 1961: p. 102.

water mains, sewers, and finished streets, primarily because schools were entirely financed through city-wide taxes and bonds. The general pattern was to start with a small school, enlarge it, and then usually replace it. In all the peripheral wards, where the school-age population grew steadily, facilities were chronically overcrowded and new construction never seemed to keep up with the increase in students.

The particular social and economic character of Milwaukee affected the city-building process in a number of important ways. The relatively level topography throughout most of the city, combined with the industrial configuration in the Menomonee Valley, reduced dependence on public transportation.[9] The exceptionally high percentage of the work force in industrial and mechanical occupations further served to reduce reliance on the streetcar, while many white-collar workers often enjoyed shorter hours and better pay, enabling them to move further from the business district. These factors may help to explain why Milwaukee was so densely settled, ranking third in persons per acre in 1910.[10] The mechanics, construction workers, and factory laborers were as eager for a decent environment as any group; but with less funds available, they settled for narrower lots, rear dwellings, double-deckers, and doubling-up to achieve a minimum goal. Such factors minimized the role of the streetcar networks and particularly the role of crosstown service, in the sorting out process.

Milwaukee was also unusual in its ethnic mix. Only two foreign-born groups predominated in the city and they each took over a whole section for themselves. Relatively few Irish, Italians, or Jews settled in Milwaukee, and the black population was minute before 1940. Had Milwaukee contained a larger number of more equally sized ethnic groups it might have developed clusters of ethnic neighborhoods and more heterogeneity within the housing stock of each of its sections.

We do not know nearly enough about the values and aspirations of the different immigrant groups of the nineteenth century to say with certainty how a particular ethnic mix affected a city's residental pattern. Contemporaries considered Germans to be an especially "home-loving" group. Social workers Robert Woods and Albert Kennedy, in their study of Boston workingclass communities, noted the Germans' "ambition for small homes with gardens."[11] Bayrd Still, in his history of Milwaukee,

---

9 U.S. Bureau of the Census, 1905: pp. 19, 25, 26.

10 McClellan and Junkersfield, Inc., 1928: 1: pp. 1, 5, 7.

11 Woods and Kennedy, 1969: pp. 124, 132; see also Glasco, 1977: pp. 132-133; Conzen, 1976: pp. 78-84.

TABLE 44

MILWAUKEE'S RANK AMONG CITIES OVER 200,000,
1910 ON SELECTED MEASURES

Population	12
Metropolitan Area Population	15
Percentage Increase in Population, 1880–1910	7
Value of Manufactured Product, 1909[a]	10
Value Added By Manufacture, 1909[a]	11
Value Added per Capita[b]	7
Percentage of Work Force in all Manufacturing and Mechanical Occupations, Males Only	2
Percentage of Work Force in White-Collar Clerical Occupations	15
Percentage of Population Foreign-Born	9
Percentage of Population of Foreign Stock	1*
Percentage of Population Under 15 years of Age	4*
Percentage of Population Under 5 years of Age	8
Persons per Acre	3
Persons per Dwelling	15
Percentage of Homes Owned	8
Streetcar Rides per Inhabitant, 1902	21
Crude Death Rate per Thousand, 1900–1909 Average	23

[a] Based on all cities ranked by largest value of product.
[b] Based on value added 1909 and population 1910.
* Tied for same rank.
  Sources: Tables 2 and 3; U.S. Bureau of the Census, 1912:
1: pp. 73–75, 178, 826, 828, 1007, 1313; 1912a: 8: p. 84; 1912c:
p. 12.

considered both the Germans and the Polish immigrants eager for homeownership, and the incidence of homeownership in urban America was far higher than in any European country. We do know that home-ownership was a principal device for social mobility for the nineteenth-century working class in the United States because it provided an important measure of financial security.[12] Woods and Kennedy realized this in their analysis of immigrants emerging from poverty into the lower middle class :

12 Still, 1948: p. 396; U.S. Congress, Senate, 1911: pp. 265-266; Wis. Bureau of Labor and Industrial Statistics, 1906: p. 315. Compare with the findings of Barton, 1975: pp. 101-104, 121; Thernstrom, 1964: pp. 137, 160, 162; Gitelman, 1974: pp. 64, 90, 98; Byington, 1910: pp. 55, 155; Bodnar, 1976: p. 49. For an alternate view, see Thernstrom, 1973: pp. 101-102; Luria, 1976: pp. 261-274.

Ownership of property is one of the surest indications that emergence is an emergence indeed. The lust for land and building constitutes a stage through through which all newcomers go. A house is large enough to signalize achievement in the most forceful way. It has a quality that bolsters a man with his neighbors as no other small ownership does. It furnishes an extremely valuable training in acquisition, and has great utility as automatically interesting the owner in government, neighborhood, and the general community situation as nothing else does.[13]

The important question is to what extent, if any, Germans and Poles were more eager for homeownership than other groups. Milwaukee had an exceptionally high rate of homeownership. In 1910 it ranked eighth on that scale among cities of 200,000 or more.[14]

Another critical issue is the role of city size and the composition of the housing stock in social mobility. In the very largest cities multi-family housing was an essential and rational accommodation to high land costs and the need of the work force to be near the employment concentrations. Multi-family housing meant a higher proportion of rental units in the housing stock. Double- and triple-deckers and small tenements could still be purchased by resident owners or small investors in the neighborhood, but the investor perforce needed larger sums for the downpayment. The relationship between the housing stock and social mobility, as measured by increased wealth, needs considerably more study in a greater number of urban settings.

MILWAUKEE AND ITS NEIGHBORHOODS
IN THE TWENTIETH CENTURY

The history of Milwaukee during the twentieth century mirrors that of American cities generally, but each city has its unique elements, and Milwaukee is no exception. Some of its deviations from the general patterns are minor, while others account for Milwaukee's particular adjustment to the changes of the century. Four trends characterize the city's twentieth-century experience:

(1) a continued growth of manufacturing until after mid-century, followed by an accelerating deindustrialization;

(2) a shift in the composition of the population to include a

---

13 Woods and Kennedy, 1969: p. 39.

14 Simon, 1971: p. 107; U.S. Bureau of the Census, 1912: 1 : p. 1313.

substantial minority of African Americans and Hispanics;

(3) an accelerated suburbanization that annexation could not overcome;

(4) a political tradition of efficiency and stability.[15]

The population of Milwaukee continued to grow, albeit unevenly, until it peaked at 740,000 in 1960. From 1960 to 1990 the city experienced a net decline of 113,000 residents. The population fell most substantially in the 1970s when it sustained an 11 percent decline, but stabilized in the 1980s with a net decline of only 1.3 percent or 8,200 people. In addition, its share of the region's population declined sharply. Using a consistent four-county definition of the metropolitan area, in 1920 the city housed 73 percent of the four-county area population. Since then the city's share has slipped steadily; by 1990 its share of the metropolitan area was down to 44 percent.

In 1990 Milwaukee was the 17th largest city in the country, a drop from 13th in 1940, but up from 18th in 1980. In 1990 its population was somewhat younger than most, with a median age of 30.3 years. The city

TABLE 45
POPULATION OF MILWAUKEE AND METROPOLITAN AREA
1920-1990

	Populaton of Milwaukee	Population of Metropolitan Area	Percent of Metropolitan Area in City
1920	457,147	624,109	73.6
1930	578,249	821,566	70.4
1940	587,472	877,044	70.0
1950	637,392	1,014,211	62.9
1960	741,324	1,278,856	58.0
1970	717,372	1,403,884	51.1
1980	636,295	1,397,020	45.6
1990	628,088	1,432,149	43.9

Note: Current metropolitan area definition is used for consistency: Milwaukee, Ozaukee, Washington, and Waukesha Counties. Sources: U.S. Bureau of the Census, 1922, 1932, 1942, 1952a, 1962, 1972, 1983, 1993.

---

15 The best recent overview of twentieth- century Milwaukee is Orum, 1995.

ranked high in the proportion of high school graduates among its adult population but low in the percentage of college graduates.

Since the 1870s manufacturing was the bedrock of Milwaukee's economy, and remained the engine of growth from 1920 to 1950. Its leading industrial sectors were electrical and non-electrical machinery, transportation equipment, food processing, primary metals, and fabricated metals.[16] Deindustrialization began slightly later in Milwaukee than other Great Lakes cities. Manufacturing jobs began to erode in the 1960s, although in 1970 Milwaukee still ranked second among the twenty largest metropolitan areas on percentage of its work force in manufacturing.[17] The erosion continued in the 1970s, but was not nearly as severe as elsewhere. In the 1980s manufacturing employment fell by a third, but the magnitude of loss was less than Buffalo, Cleveland, or Detroit.[18]

The recession of the early 1980s hit the city particularly hard. In the late 1970s manufacturing jobs had actually risen, only to drop by 22 percent in the early 1980s. For the first time in the twentieth century service jobs exceeded those in manufacturing.[19] It was the growth of the service sector which accounted for the population stability of the 1980s.

TABLE 46
DECLINE IN MANUFACTURING EMPLOYMENT
IN GREAT LAKES CITIES, 1950-1990

Percentage Change in Number of Persons in Manufacturing:	Milwaukee	Buffalo	Chicago	Cleveland	Detroit
1950-1960	+ 2.0	-18.0	-15.1	-16.6	-34.4
1960-1970	-14.8	-22.7	-11.9	-22.1	-12.0
1970-1980	-13.5	-36.5	-25.9	-33.9	-43.9
1980-1990	-32.3	-39.3	-31.5	-40.7	-39.1
Number of Persons in Manufacturing, 1990	60,991	21,201	225,307	42.137	68,830
Percent of Work Force in Manufacturing, 1990	22.2	16.2	18.7	23.1	20.5

Sources: U.S. Bureau of the Census, 1952a; 1962; 1972; 1983; 1993.

16 U.S. Bureau of the Census, 1963: vol III, pp. 50-58.

17 Schmandt et al, 1971: p. 9.

18 Orum, 1995: pp. 125; Norman, 1989: p. 181.

19 Norman, 1989: p. 192; Wilkerson, 1991: p. A1.

Pulled along by such firms as Northwest Mutual Life Insurance Company and Manpower, office employment and new office buildings helped carry the city through the difficult economic transition. Most of the new construction occurred on the east side which had always been the financial core of the central business district, while the downtown retail district on West Wisconsin Avenue deteriorated physically and economically. The Grand Avenue Mall, a successful Rouse Company three-block downtown shopping mall, stemmed the decline of the retail district and may have encouraged other central business district investment.[20]

Ethnic diversity was a key element of Milwaukee's population from the beginning. However, after the restriction of European immigration in the 1920s there was little further change in the ethnic stock of the population for forty years. African Americans were a part of Milwaukee's population since the late nineteenth century, but their numbers remained quite small until the 1950s. In the first great wave of northward migration, in the 1910s and 1920s, blacks largely overlooked Milwaukee, gravitating instead to such centers as Chicago, Detroit, and St. Louis. In 1940 African-Americans accounted for only 1.6 percent of the city's population. However, during the 1940s the black population jumped by 144 percent to almost 23,000. The number of African Americans tripled in the 1950s and doubled again in the 1960s. Their share of the total

TABLE 47

AFRICAN AMERICAN POPULATION OF MILWAUKEE,
1940-1990

	Population	Percent of City Population
1940	9,295	1.6
1950	21,772	3.4
1960	62,458	8.4
1970	105,088	14.7
1980	145,832	22.9
1990	189,408	30.1

Note: Figures for 1940 are for all non-whites; since 1950 for African Americans.
Sources: Tien, 1962: p. 25; U.S. Bureau of the Census, 1972; 1983, 1993.

20 Norman, 1989: p. 193.

also rose rapidly as whites departed for the suburbs.

In the early decades of the century Milwaukee's small black community clustered in an old and deteriorated neighborhood to the northwest of the business district. From this core the population grew slowly and expanded outward. In the early 1930s a city housing survey identified a blighted area, labeled simply "the Negro District," running north from W. Juneau to W. Garfield Street between N. 4th St. and N. 11th St. [21] In 1930 that district was 45 percent black. The housing stock was deteriorated and many homes lacked central heat; 10 percent of the dwellings had no indoor plumbing. The area was characterized by both high density and high vacancy rates. This was not the only neighborhood of blighted conditions, but it was the core of the black ghetto. [22]

As the city's African American community grew in size, it expanded north and west from this core. By 1990 the black ghetto had expanded to include all of Wards 20 and 22 and beyond. [23] Rapid expansion of the ghetto did not, however, mean that segregation declined. Although there was always a transition zone at the edge of the expanding ghetto, such integrated areas quickly resegregated. Despite its small black community in 1940, the city was extremely segregated and remained so over the next fifty years. The index of dissimilarity between African Americans and whites at the block level was 92.9 in 1940 and fell only to 83.7 in 1970. [24] Using tract level data, the index of dissimilarity for 1970 was 66.9, rising to 76.6 in 1980 before falling slightly to 73.7 in 1990. This pattern of increased segregation in the 1970s and slight decline in the 1980s reflected a national trend. Equally revealing was Milwaukee's ranking among large cities on the index value. In 1970 and 1980 Milwaukee ranked 17th among the largest cities, rising to 15th in 1990. In 1990, Cleveland, Chicago, Philadelphia, and Atlanta all had higher indices of dissimilarity. [25]

Several recent studies have characterized Milwaukee as the most segregated city in the country. However, data that support this conclu-

---

21 On the ward map on page 2 that district would have been in the lower half of Ward 6 with a spill-over into the eastern corner of Wards 9 and 10.

22 Milw. Housing Commission. 1933: pp. 12-16.

23 Milw. Dept. of City Development. 1992. p. 9.

24 Massey and Denton, 1993: p. 47.

25 Kasarda, 1993: pp. 122-124. The value of the index is greatly affected by the size of the unit. The smaller the unit the higher the number will be. The indices in ch. 2 are based on wards; there were twenty-three in 1910. In 1990 there were 229 wholly or partly in the city of Milwaukee.

sion are based on the metropolitan area rather than the city proper. In 1990, 97.3 percent of metropolitan area blacks lived in the city. By such measures of segregation as indices of centralization and concentration, Milwaukee ranked first in 1980 among large northern metropolitan areas. Those measures indicate that the black population is relatively close to the city's core and occupies a relatively small land area. To some extent, these measures reflect the historic high density of the nineteenth century city. They may say more about the suburbs than about the city itself. This segregation level may also be a function of the relatively late arrival of blacks to Milwaukee. The index of dissimilarity by census tract which ranks Milwaukee fifteenth among the large cities is a more consistent and reliable standard, but by any measure Milwaukee was an extremely segregated city.[26]

The rapid growth of the city's black community in the 1950s and 1960s caused considerable racial tension. As in other cities Milwaukee officials went to considerable lengths to perpetuate *de facto* segregation. Particularly egregious was the School Board's practice of "intact busing," whereby entire "classes" of black students from ghetto neighborhoods were bused to schools in white neighborhoods that had empty classrooms. The black children were kept segregated in the classroom, lunchroom and during recess. In response to protests by the black community, the Board in 1965 said integration was "administratively unfeasible." [27]

In 1967 and 1968 racial tensions manifested in two incidents that brought the city some national attention. During the tumultuous summer of 1967 Milwaukee had a brief urban riot. It lasted five hours and cost three lives. A full scale riot was short-circuited when the national guard was quickly deployed and the mayor, Henry Maier, imposed a ten-day curfew.[28] The same summer a local priest, Father James Groppi, led a march of black teens to Kosciuszko Park in the heart of old Ward 14. The demonstrators were chased out of the south side by an angry mob. Groppi soon followed with open housing demonstrations for two hundred consecutive evenings. The city and the suburbs eventually passed mildly worded open housing ordinances which, as we have seen, never had much impact on the pattern of

26 Norman, 1989: p. 179; Orum, 1995: p. 133; Massey and Denton, 1993: pp. 64-76; for measures of the segregation of the poor and socially disadvantaged in Milwaukee relative to other large cities see Kasarda, 1993: pp. 111-124.

27 Bernard, 1990: pp. 177-178. The case went to court, but a final ruling was not handed down until 1978, by which time the parties had accepted an out of court settlement.

28 U.S. Report of the National Advisory Committee on Civil Disorders, p. 524.

segregation.[29]

Like all other major cities, Milwaukee experienced substantial suburbanization in the twentieth century, and, like most cities, attempted to include this population and its affluent tax base in the city. Milwaukee was actually much more successful than some other cities of its size, although by the 1960s it, too, was surrounded by incorporated suburbs. In the 1920s greater use of the automobile accelerated outward migration, causing Milwaukee to focus more aggressively than before on annexation. Milwaukee was successful in attracting property owners at the periphery, many of whom were subdividers and speculators, to agree to annexation with the promise of extending city services. Milwaukee's annexation efforts between 1920 and 1940 yielded impressive gains as the city grew from 22 to 44 square miles; however, it lost several efforts to annex the more populous and affluent communities or to merge the city and the county. From 1940-60 the city again doubled in size to 91 square miles.[30]

The state of Wisconsin effectively ended Milwaukee's annexation drive with two decisions in the 1950s. The first, a state Supreme Court decision, required Milwaukee to sell water to adjacent municipalities, denying the city its principal leverage for annexation. The second key decision, an act of the legislature passed by one vote, permitted sparsely settled townships to incorporate, thus making further annexations almost impossible.[31]

Overall, the developments of the post-war era left Milwaukee with a declining tax base, limited job opportunities, particularly for minorities, and an aging and increasingly obsolete physical plant of homes, factories, offices, stores, and transportation systems. In an effort to remain competitive with other cities and, increasingly with its own suburban communities, the city government and local elites made some efforts to address those developments. As in other areas, most of what was done in Milwaukee was similar to agendas and approaches taken elsewhere. In all these endeavors the city government played a major role, with political and logistical support from major business interests.[32]

---

29 Norman, 1989: pp. 188-89; Bernard, 1990: pp. 178-181.

30 Tien, 1962: p. 22; Fleischmann, 1988: pp. 152-158; see Teaford, 1979: pp. 97-100 and passim for a general treatment of municipal annexation.

31 Bernard, 1990: p. 175; Fleischmann, 1988: pp.158-170; Orum, 1995: pp. 119-121.

32 The involvement of business leaders in setting the post-war agenda is most fully discussed in Orum, 1995: ch. 7. For comparable examples in other cities, see Lubove, 1969 and Hirsch, 1983.

Although Milwaukee had one of the country's largest and most successful municipal socialist parties, its twentieth century political tradition has been cautious and conservative. Bold experimentation has not been the hallmark of Milwaukee government on almost any front. The consequences, however, have not necessarily been detrimental. The socialists did leave one important legacy in Milwaukee city government: a tradition of honest, efficient administration. Milwaukee politics was also characterized by remarkable stability. Three mayors, Daniel Hoan (1916-40), Frank Zeidler (1948-60), and Henry Maier (1960-88) dominated city hall through most of the century. Although Hoan was elected as a Socialist, Zeidler was the most liberal of the three, and his positions may have cost him the office. The Socialists also bequeathed a tradition of pay-as-you-go government. Into the early 1950s Milwaukee had no bonded debt.[33]

In the late 1940s, to combat manifest and incipient decline, the city's business and financial elites formed the Greater Milwaukee Council (GMC). Then and later the GMC focused on capital projects to preserve and enhance the central business district and the city's attractiveness for business. Their initial agenda advocated borrowing for a baseball stadium, an indoor sports arena, a museum, a zoo, and an expressway from the airport to downtown, goals which were largely met. Later they focused heavily on freeway construction.[34] In many ways the GMC dominated the city's agenda for decades, but it did not devote much attention to housing conditions or neighborhood life in general. In the 1960s they formed a bi-racial civic group to promote minority hiring, but it did not address any fundamental issues, and little came of the effort.[35]

The city did undertake some urban renewal projects on the west side in the deteriorated neighborhoods just north and west of the central business district. As in most such projects, demolition proceeded with alacrity while replacement languished for years.[36] The successful Grand Avenue Mall project highlights the limitations of urban renewal that focuses on the business district and is dominated by local elites. While the mall project secured adequate funding and was completed fairly rapidly, neither the GMC nor the city administration were willing to

---

33 Orum, 1995: p. 169; Schmandt et. al., 1971: pp. 141-142.

34 Schmandt et al, 1971: p. 102; Orum, 1995: p. 275; Norman, 1989: pp. 178-179.

35 Norman, 1989: pp. 178-79, 189-191; Orum, 1995: p. 275; Bernard, 1990: p. 172.

36 Schmandt et al, 1971: p. 168.

invest heavily in neighborhoods.[37]

The primary reason for demolition of homes in the post-war period, in Milwaukee and other cities, was not urban renewal but highway construction. In the 1960s an interstate highway network was built into and through Milwaukee. The North-South Expressway eliminated the square block between 7th and 8th streets through the entire length of the north side. An east-west freeway running along the edge of the Menomonee Valley removed less housing. However, the state also cleared a strip of land 1 1/2 miles in length and a square block wide between North Avenue and Meinecke Street for a proposed "Park West Corridor." This project was abandoned, but the land lay vacant for decades. Most of it was still vacant in the mid-1990s. Of course, most of those removed for the corridor were African Americans.[38]

In a number of cities, public housing was an essential concomitant to urban renewal. However, Milwaukee never built an extensive inventory of public housing. During the depression the WPA sponsored a 518 unit project on open land in the northwest section at Sherman Boulevard and N. 47th Street. The city moved very slowly on public housing and built fewer units than other comparably sized cities. It preferred to build first for veterans and later for the elderly rather than for low income families. Resistance came from local builders and conservatives who saw socialism. By the mid-1950s they were joined by working class and middle class whites fearful that public housing units would attract African Americans, particularly to their neighborhoods. Most of the public housing built in the city, therefore, was on scattered sites. In the long run the absence of a dense cluster of public housing units may have been a positive development for the city.[39]

In sum, twentieth-century Milwaukee was a socially and politically conservative city, despite its nominally socialist heritage. It remained a heavy industry city until the last quarter of the century. Perhaps because no single industry dominated as in Detroit, it was more successful at shifting to a service economy. While it was also more successful in adding to its territory than some of its peer cities, eventually the affluent automobile-oriented suburbs were able to block its growth. The minority population arrived later, and perhaps for that reason, located more

37 Norman, 1989: p. 195; Orum, 1995: pp. 128-130.

38 Orum, 1995: pp. 128-130; Norman, 1989: pp. 189-191.

39 Schmandt et. al., 1971: pp. 166-67; Bernard, 1990: p. 173; Beckley, 1978: pp. 144-160; Milw. Dept. of City Development, 1994; on the creation of a public housing ghetto, see the Chicago experience in Hirsch, 1983.

completely in the city proper than that of comparable cities. Milwaukee never built as many public housing units nor demolished as much sound housing for "urban renewal" as many other comparable communities. How then did the residential neighborhoods, built for turn-of-the-century families, fare in these changing circumstances?

If the economic anchors which attract people to a location are not ripped away and the housing stock has the adaptability to meet the changing needs of its population, a neighborhood can retain its character and enjoy population stability. A housing stock can be upgraded and modernized. While older spacious homes with attractive amenities located in a prestigious section are often able to hold their status, such conditions are no guarantee of stability and reinvestment. Just as the three neighborhoods examined here housed very different segments of the city's population in distinct kinds of housing, each changed in very different ways during the course of the twentieth century. The Ward 18 area remained attractive to a middle to upper middle class population; its housing stock consequently remained sound with high property values. If there was some slippage in its prestige, it underwent a modest "gentrification" in the 1980s. Ward 14 retained its working class population; the property owners invested in upgrading and modernizing their modest homes. The Ward 20-22 area, however, experienced a dramatic change from a lower middle class zone to one that housed the bulk of Milwaukee's poor families. The condition of its housing deteriorated badly, although values remained high because of its proximity to the center of town.

To assess how the three neighborhoods adapted to the changing social and economic circumstances, we can turn to census tract data reported for Milwaukee since 1940. The boundaries of the tracts do not entirely coincide with the turn-of-the-century wards, but the match is close (see Appendix C).

Between 1910 and 1940 the social and housing character of the Ward 20-22 area changed little; the area remained home to families of the lower middle class and working-class population. Measures of the housing stock indicate that the neighborhood was close to the city-wide norms for property values and percentage of units owner occupied. The percentage of persons employed as craftsmen and machine operators, core manufacturing occupations, was slightly higher than the city average. In 1950 the median household income in the area was $3,409 which was slightly above the city-wide median.

Subsequently, however, the area underwent a complete change in character. From a virtually all-white neighborhood in 1940, it became almost entirely African American, with the racial turnover occurring primarily in the 1960s. By 1970 the district was 59 percent black; this figure, however, masked considerable internal variation. The six tracts closest to the business district, those south of Auer St. and east of 24th St., were 90 percent or more African American while the five tracts furthest west and north were 90 percent or more white. By 1990, however, the resegregation of the entire areas was complete: the two most westerly tracts were over 80 percent black, all the others were over 90 percent. In the 1950s and 1960s the city's African American population grew rapidly and, needing affordable housing like everyone else, expanded steadily north and west from its historic ghetto area. The North-South Expressway and the Park West Corridor accelerated the population turnover in the 1960s. Seventy percent of the families displaced for the North-South Expressway were black.[40]

The social characteristics of the population mirrored national trends. The black community as a whole was extremely hard hit by the deindustrialization of the 1970s and 1980s. Household income for the area as a percentage of the city median fell steadily from 92 percent in 1940 to only 58 percent, or $13,725, in 1990 when over half of the population lived in households with incomes below the poverty line. The labor force participation rate for both men and women age 16 and over was well below the city average. Over half of the households were headed by women. The area also had the largest percentage of children under 18. Whereas the share of children fell in the other areas, it rose in Ward 20-22.[41]

The condition of the housing stock reflected the social turnover in population. Although the number of overcrowded units and units lacking full plumbing declined over the decades, there was, nevertheless, substantial deterioration in the housing stock. As the area became home to an economically disadvantaged population, an increasing number of buildings became abandoned. The city pursued an aggressive policy of demolition of abandoned buildings to prevent the spread of blight. As a result the number of dwelling units fell between 1970 and 1990 by 25 percent. Despite this policy, in 1990 12.4 percent of the dwelling units were vacant, more than double the city wide figure of 5.4

---

40 House, 1970: p. 76.

41 U.S. Bureau of the Census, 1993: part CPH-3-231A; Milw. Dept. of City Development, 1992: pp. 15, 19, 24; Edari, 1978: pp. 86-111; Wilkerson, 1991: p. A1.

percent. [42]

The value of single family units also reflects the shift in population. In 1940 the median value of owner occupied units was 84.5 percent of the city average, but this slid to 53 percent in 1990. In contrast, however, the estimated median gross rent remained very stable at close to the city median, falling only from 106 percent of the city average to 97 percent over the fifty years. This stability in rent levels may reflect the racially segregated housing market in which blacks are still confined to certain segments of the city.

To walk through the area in the mid-1990s leaves an impression of an obsolete neighborhood, although not one of desperation. Along most of the old commercial strips the stores are boarded up or empty. On the residential blocks the condition of the homes is uneven. Many are in need of repairs or a fresh coat of paint. Perhaps the most overt change since 1970 are the empty lots found on each block where the city demolished abandoned homes. Unfortunately, most of those lots are overgrown with weeds; their most prominent feature is a sign warning against dumping. In a few blocks in the oldest sections of Ward 20 the combination of empty lots and boarded up buildings betray marks of serious decay. However, urbanists familiar with the such neighborhoods as Pittsburgh's Hill District, North Philadelphia, the South Bronx, or Boston's Roxbury, would find these streets, with their modest yards and mature trees, a much less bleak environment. The City Housing Authority has taken over a number of properties as scattered site housing, but even some of those were boarded up in 1994. [43]

Although the houses in Ward 14 were much smaller than in Wards 20-22 and two units were often carved out of homes intended for one family, the neighborhood enjoyed much more stability of population and housing values. In 1940 Ward 14 was still very much a working-class district. Sixty percent of employed adults were craftsmen, production workers, or machine and transportation operators, a rate almost 1.5 times the city average. Only 6.8 per cent of adults had completed high school. In 1950 median family income was $3,300, very close to the city-wide median.

---

42   The vacancy figure includes units available for rent or sale as well as those abandoned or boarded up. Since the rentability of units was unknown, the total number of vacancies is reported. It is notable, however, that 60 percent of all the boarded up units in the city were in this area. U.S. Bureau of the Census, 1993: Table 9.

43   Milw. Dept. of City Development, 1994.

Fig. 35.   1756 N. 25th Street.   Housing Authority "Scatter Site" property, 1994.
Picture, 1994.

Fig. 36.   2857 N. 25th Street.   Housing Authority "Scatter Site" property, 1994.
Picture, 1994.

TABLE 48
SOCIAL AND HOUSING INDICATORS, 20th-22nd WARD AREA, 1940-1990[a]

	1940	1960	1980	1990
Population	67,889	58,758	47,846	44,653
Percent Black	.04	22.7	85.2	93.2
Percent Hispanic[b]	--	.4	2.1	1.0
Percent age 5-14	14.0	23.5	24.1	24.4
Percent Adults with Four Years of High School or More	17.0	30.8	47.4	49.2
Ratio to City-wide Percent Adults with Four Years of High School or More	.758	.774	.745	.688
Median Household Income[c]	$3,409[d]	$6,075	$ 11,581	$13,725
Ratio to City-wide Median Household Income	1.02	.911	.722	.581
Percent of Workers Craftsmen or Machine Operators	48.2	45.1	38.5	30.5
Ratio to City-Wide Percent of Craftsmen and Machine Operators	1.17	1.16	1.1	1.23
Percent of Persons Five and Over at Same House Five Years Earlier	n.a.	48.75	50.0	48.7
Ratio to City Percent of Persons Five and Over at Same House Five Years Earlier	n.a.	1.03	.99	.92
Number of Dwelling Units	19,693	19,506	15,483	14,347
Persons per Dwelling Unit	3.45	3.01	3.09	3.1
Percent of Occupied Dwelling Units Owner Occupied	36.9	42.8	34.2	27.7
Ratio to City-wide Percent of Occupied Dwelling Units Owner Occupied	.873	.884	.724	.653
Percent of all Dwelling Units Lacking Full Plumbing[e]	10.2	6.8	1.8	.7
Percent of all Occupied Units with more than 1.5 Persons per room	1.2	n.a.	1.4	.31
Percent all Units Vacant	1.8	3.9	8.6	12.4
Median Value Owner Occupied Units	$3,450	$11,015	$21,508	$28,203
Ratio to City Median Value Owner Occupied Units	.845	.729	.472	.527
Median Gross Rent	$39	$87	$247	$407
Ratio to City Median Gross Rent	1.06	1.00	1.04	.974

n.a.--Not Available; double dash indicates less than .1 percent.
Sources: U. S. Bureau of the Census, 1942a, 1952, 1962, 1983, 1993.

a. See Appendix C for list of Census Tracts included in this table.

b. For 1940, persons born in Mexico; for 1960, persons born in Puerto Rico, persons of Puerto Rican parentage, and persons of Mexican parentage.

c. Medians for interval data for this and similar variables were calculated by a method which distributes the observations across the class; see Kirk, 1990: pp. 89-93.

d. Income data was not reported in 1940; figure is for income of families and unrelated individuals in 1949.

e. The 1960 Census reports made a distinction between "sound," "Deteriorating," and "Dilapidated" units. For "Sound" and "deteriorating" units, those lacking full plumbing were reported separately; for "dilapidated" units they were not. In this count, all "dilapidated" units are counted as lacking full plumbing.

Homeownership was obviously a high priority of the first generation of families in Ward 14, and in 1940, 34 percent of the units were
owner occupied, a rate slightly above the city average. However,
homeownership continued to have its costs in personal privacy, as 44
percent of the dwelling units shared bathroom facilities, a level more
than twice the city average. In addition, overcrowding persisted with 4.3
percent of the dwelling units averaging 1.5 or more persons per room.
On two key indicators of privacy, crowding and bathroom facilities, the
Ward 14 area ranked well below the city average. The value of owner
occupied units and the estimated gross rent both ranked twenty to
twenty-five percent below the city average.

Through the 1970s the Ward 14 area remained exceptionally
stable in both population characteristics and housing stock. The most
remarkable development was the substantial upgrading in the quality of
housing conditions. The percentage of units overcrowded and the
percentage of units lacking full plumbing both fell below one percent. As
the quality improved so did the housing value. In 1940 the average gross
rent was $30, 82 percent of the city-wide average. By 1980 the gross rent
had risen to 91 percent of the city-wide average. The value of owner
occupied units, although rising from $3,060 to $35,833 did not keep pace
with the rest of the city, falling from three-quarters to two-thirds of the
city average.

Part of the decongestion was a function of the aging process both
of the neighborhood and its residents. The area renewed itself as enough
young families were attracted to stay or to settle so that the social and
economic character remained stable. Smaller families further reduced
crowding over time.

For over thirty years the area remained remarkably homogeneous
in its population characteristics. Median household income did slip from
91 percent of the city average in 1950 to 81 percent in 1990. The area
remained home to a disproportionately large number of factory workers.
In both 1940 and 1990 the percent of the work force engaged in craft
production and machine operations was 1.5 times the city average.
There was a dramatic increase in the percent of adults with at least a
high school education, rising from 7.2 to 57.4 percent. Turnover in the
area was lower than the city average. In 1960, 56 percent of the
population was at the same address five years earlier, a proportion almost
twenty percent above the city average and substantially higher than the
other two study areas. In subsequent decades the figure fell closer to the
city-wide average, but remained higher than Wards 18 or 20-22.

At the turn of the century this was Milwaukee's primary Polish neighborhood. As the city expanded further south the Polish community spread out, but the predominant Polish character of this area remained strong until the 1980s. In 1960 and 1970 the Polish foreign stock of the Ward remained high. In 1970 19 percent of the population had parents born in Poland as compared to 4 percent of the entire city. Not until 1980 did the census report information on ethnic ancestry beyond parents' place of birth. This information is only an approximation since people could and did list multiple ancestries. Nonetheless, the data reveal a continued, but somewhat diminished presence of a Polish community in the Ward. In 1980, 43 percent of the residents reported a Polish ancestry and in 1990, 30 percent did so. The dense network of churches and parochial schools served as a major community anchor along with such near-by industrial employers as Allen-Bradley.

In the 1960s Fr. James Groppi led his housing demonstrators right into the heart of Ward 14 for a rally in Kosciuszko Park. Police kept an angry mob of residents from inflicting serious injury on the outnumbered demonstrators. If the city's black population needed any reminder that the south side was unfriendly territory, the episode certainly filled that mission. But while the number of blacks in the area remained very small, there has been a substantial increase in the Hispanic population.

Most of Milwaukee's Hispanic community is of Mexican origin. In 1960 the principal cluster of Mexican Americans was located around Walker's Point, the oldest neighborhood on the south side in its northeast corner. From this ghetto the community slowly expanded to the west and south. In 1980 the Spanish Origins community had expanded into the northern tier of tracts of the Ward 14 area, those tracts north of Becher St. By 1990 the Ward 14 area was 24 percent Hispanic, but as with the Ward 20-22 area earlier, this average disguised considerable internal variation. The two most northerly tracts, those between Mitchell and Becher, were 38 and 45 percent Hispanic respectively, while the three most southerly tracts, those below Lincoln and Arthur Avenues, were between 10 and 13 percent Hispanic. Examining the population trends since 1970 and the aging population and housing stock, the evidence would suggest that the entire district was in the process of resegregating as an Hispanic neighborhood.

The blocks south of Lincoln looked virtually unchanged from 1970 to the mid 1990s. These blocks had larger single and two family flats than those to the north. The properties clearly had been well maintained. There were no boarded up homes and no vacant lots. Nonetheless, in the mid-1990s for-sale signs were sprouting on almost every block south of Lincoln Avenue, indicative of future residential turnover.

TABLE 49

SOCIAL AND HOUSING INDICATORS, 14th WARD AREA
1940-1990[a]

	1940	1960	1980	1990
Population	36,018	27,692	20,747	21,831
Percent Black	.03	.07	2.0	1.5
Percent Hispanic[b]	--	.89	11.0	24.0
Percent Age 5-14	17.3	19.7	11.6	17.4
Percent Adults with Four Years of High School or More	7.2	23.7	45.8	57.4
Ratio to City-wide Percent Adults with Four Years or more High School	.327	.597	.72	.803
Median Household Income[c]	$ 3,300[d]	$ 6,057	$ 14,122	$ 19,231
Ratio to City-wide Median Household Income	.98	.909	.881	.814
Percent of Workers Craftsmen or operators	60.8	48.0	40.3	36.1
Percent of Persons Age Five and over at Same Address Five Years Earlier	n.a.	56.0	50.2	50.0
Ratio to City Percent of Persons Five and over at Same Address Five Years	n.a.	1.18	1.0	.95
Number of Dwelling Units	8,964	8,932	8,384	8,537
Persons per Dwelling Unit	4.02	3.1	2.48	2.56
Percent of Occupied Dwelling Units Owner Occupied	34.6	44.9	39.4	34.0
Ratio to City-wide Percent of Occupied Dwelling Units Owner Occupied	1.075	.928	.826	.803
Percent of all Dwelling Units Lacking Full Plumbing[e]	44.3	17.3	2.76	.65
Percent of all Occupied Units with more than 1.5 Persons per Room	4.3	n/a	.79	.31
Percent all Units Vacant	1.5	4.9	.05	7.3
Median Value, Owner Occupied Units	$ 3,060	$ 11,114	$ 32,416	$ 35,833
Ratio to City wide Median Value, Owner Occupied Units	.749	.736	.712	.670
Median Gross Rent	$ 30.00	$ 67.00	$ 216.00	$ 373.00
Ratio to City Median Gross Rent	.819	.77	.908	.892

n.a.--Not Available; double dash indicates less than .1 percent.

Sources: U.S. Bureau of the Census, 1942a, 1952, 1962, 1983, 1993.

a. See Appendix C for list of tracts included in this table.

b. For 1940 persons born in Mexico, for 1960 persons born in Puerto Rico, persons of Puerto Rican parentage, and persons of Mexican parentage.

c. Medians for interval data for this and similar variables was calculated by a method which distributes the observations across the class; see Kirk, 1990: pp. 89-93.

d. Income data was not reported in 1940; figure is for income of families and unrelated individuals in 1949.

e. The 1960 Census reports made a distinction between "sound," "Deteriorating," and "Dilapidated" units. For "Sound" and "deteriorating" units, those lacking full plumbing were reported separately; for "dilapidated" units they were not. In this count, all "dilapidated" units are counted as lacking full plumbing.

The neighborhood served for one hundred years as a principal residential zone for the workers in Milwaukee's heavy industry. As the city deindustrialized the anchors to the neighborhood began to fall away. The housing stock had been upgraded and the small homes and rental units proved serviceable to the Polish working class community. Much as the flats and cottages of the north side had been recycled for a newcomer population of African Americans, the modest housing of Ward 14 was being turned over to a growing Hispanic community.

Ward 18 was the most fashionable of the peripheral areas of the city in 1900 and it has been remarkably successful at retaining its population character and a quality housing stock over the course of the twentieth century, but, as with the other areas, there have been notable changes in both population and housing stock. In 1940 the Ward 18 area contained 30,189 people in 8,500 dwelling units. The value of housing in the area, both owned and rented, ranked above the city-wide medians. A higher percentage of the homes in the area were single family dwellings than in the other wards. Professionals, managers, and proprietors continued to be over-represented in the district. From the 1950s through the 1970s the district slipped somewhat in the socioeconomic position of its residents, as newer suburban communities along the Lake shore to the north siphoned off affluent white collar families. In 1950 the median family income was right at the city average, but it fell to 92 percent in 1980 before rising to 113 percent in 1990, indicative a modest "gentrification."

Three factors account for the area's stability: proximity to the lake, a high quality housing stock with large numbers of single family homes on larger than average lots, and proximity to white collar employment. The University of Wisconsin at Milwaukee, which expanded rapidly in the 1960s and 1970s, became the principal employer in the ward and a magnet for professionals. Furthermore, the boom in downtown office construction in the 1980s occurred on the east side, a short commute from the Ward 18 area.

Unlike the other two areas, Ward 18 increased the number of dwelling units even as the population declined. In 1940 the Ward 18 and Ward 20-22 areas each averaged 3.5 persons per dwelling unit. By 1990 Ward 18 had fallen to 2.19 persons per dwelling unit while Ward 20-22 fell only to 3.1. A major factor in the growth of dwelling units was the conversion of some large single homes into apartments and the construction of small apartment buildings on a number of blocks in the middle of

TABLE 50
SOCIAL AND HOUSING INDICATORS, 18th WARD AREA
1940-1990ᵃ

	1940	1960	1980	1990
Population	30,189	26,633	24,181	24,805
Percent Black	.09	.07	.07	4.0
Percent Hispanicᵇ	--	.3	2.0	2.6
Percent age 5-14	13.0	15.1	6.3	5.4
Percent Adults with four years of high school or more	20.4	65.7	98.9	89.9
Ratio to City-wide Percent Adults with four years of high school or more	.92	1.78	1.56	1.26
Median Household Incomeᶜ	$ 3,348ᵈ	$7,098	$ 14,748	$26,667
Ratio to City-wide Average Household Income	1.00	1.07	.92	1.13
Percent of Professional, Managers, Proprietors and Technicians	30.2	26.6	42.9	42.4
Percent of Persons Five and Over at Same Address Five Years Earlier	n.a.	46.9	34.2	30.5
Ratio to City Percent of Persons Five and Over at Same Address	n.a.	.992	.678	.580
Number of Dwelling Units	8,500	8.910	11,372	11,329
Persons per Dwelling Unit	3.55	2.49	2.13	2.19
Percent of Occupied Dwelling Units Owner Occupied	32.6	38.6	23.8	26.2
Ratio to City-wide Percent of Occupied Dwelling Units Owner Occupied	1.01	.798	.504	.620
Percent of all Dwelling Units Lacking Full Plumbingᵉ	10.9	.8	2.5	.82
Percent of all Occupied Units with more than 1.5 Persons per Room	2.0	n.a.	.5	. 02
Percent all Units Vacant	4.7	4.0	2.2	3.8
Median Value, Owner Occupied Units	$ 5,618	$16,821	$ 54,983	$99,301
Ratio to City Median Value Owner Occupied Units	1.38	1.11	1.21	1.86
Median Gross Rent	$46	$ 94	$ 260	$ 473
Ratio to City Median Gross Rent	1.26	1.08	1.09	1.13

n.a.--Not Available; double dash indicates less than .1 percent.
Sources: U. S. Bureau of the Census, 1942a, 1952, 1962, 1983, 1993.

a. See Appendix C for list of census tracts included in this table.

b. For 1940, persons born in Mexico; for 1960, persons born in Puerto Rico, persons of Puerto Rican parentage, and persons of Mexican parentage.

c. Medians for interval data for this and similar variables were calculated by a method which distributes the observations across the class; see Kirk, 1990: pp. 89-93.

d. Income data was not reported in 1940; figure is for income of families and unrelated individuals in 1949.

e. The 1960 Census reports made a distinction between "sound," "Deteriorating," and "Dilapidated" units. For "Sound" and "deteriorating" units, those lacking full plumbing were reported separately; for "dilapidated" units they were not. In this count, all "dilapidated" units are counted as lacking full plumbing.

the area.[44]

Of the three areas, Ward 18, as it fully developed, had more internal variation in its housing stock than either of the other areas. The oldest part of the ward, the southwest corner below North Avenue and west of Farwell Street dated from the 1860s and 1870s and focused around the abortive canal project along the Milwaukee River. The neighborhood filled with small cottages, similar to those found in Ward 14, and two-family flats.[45] In contrast, the tracts facing Lake Michigan had consistently higher housing values and a higher income population. In 1940, in each of the tracts by the Lake, 40 percent or more of all employed persons were professionals, managers, or proprietors. In 1990 the four tracts with the highest median household income were the two lakeside tracts and the two along the city's northern border. The tracts with the lowest household income, lowest value of housing, and smallest percentage of white collar workers were those in the southwest corner.[46]

The three neighborhoods examined in this study each represented the best new urban environment its first residents could afford. The goal of those residents was a modern home with adequate space inside and outside the dwelling for their families, water and sewer services, and, for many, the opportunity to become homeowners. The artisans and lower paid white-collar workers, predominantly of German origin, who filled out the northwest periphery, could usually attain this goal in a short time with a minimum of sacrifice. The area contained many two-family flats, providing some rental income for the owners and roomy apartments for families lacking the capital or the need to own. The large flats, however, did crowd the land and created a very dense neighborhood. A generation later, when the middle class residents were ready to move again to more modern, lower density neighborhoods, the homes filled with a new but relatively impoverished population. The homes which the African Americans inherited were, at least, spacious. On the south side, where rental apartments helped finance homeownership, families were forced to accept considerably less space. In the long run, however, the single family homes of Ward 14 provided an acceptable middle class environ-

---

44 For example, Frederick Street between Bradford and Newberry has a number of small apartment buildings.

45 This segment of the ward did not figure prominently in the sample data because of the manner in which the sample was constructed. Each facing block was treated the same regardless of the size of the block. The southwest corner had a relatively small number of very long blocks, while the streets west of Farwell had short blocks. Consequently, only one block in the southwest was included in the sample data.

46 See Appendix C for tract maps and comparability tables.

ment. Had the area been overbuilt at higher densities with triple-decker
flats there would have been no flexibility for conversion, consolidation
of units, and upgrading.[47]

The new neighborhoods on Milwaukee's periphery provided more
space for raising children than the older, more densely built-up areas.
Further, the opportunity for homeownership was very real and obviously
a deeply felt goal for at least part of the population, regardless of whether
it was a wise financial investment. The new housing stock and public
policy permitted an ordering of priorities in which financial security
won out over convenience and public health. The environmental self-
determination permitted each social and ethnic group to stake out its
own section of the city and finance the kind of environment it could
afford.

---

47 See the illustrations in Warner, 1962: pp. 57, 91, 96, 115, 151, for examples of the
double and triple-deckers. Many eastern cities provide examples of six family flats.

APPENDIX A.
USING THE WISCONSIN CENSUS ROLLS OF 1905

The 1905 census was the last undertaken by the state of Wisconsin; it was also the most complete, containing almost as much information as the federal manuscript schedules. For Milwaukee, the schedules are arranged by enumerating districts which coincide with voting precincts. However, the schedules do not provide house numbers and street names, so that using them at less than the precinct level requires auxiliary sources. The method I employed in this study proved quite reliable. By using the city directory as an index, I traced the path of the enumerator through his district. I took the top name on every other page of the schedules and looked it up in the city directory to obtain the house number. Since the city directory canvass did not occur at the same time as the census enumeration it was necessary to use more than one directory. I used the directories of 1904, 1905, and 1906. Because I knew the full name, occupation, and approximate location of the person I was looking for in the directory it was not difficult to locate the correct party in most cases. Some imagination was required to conceive of possible misspellings of various Polish names, but even here there were fewer problems than anticipated.

Once I located the sample block on the census schedule, I looked up the address of every name until I "followed" the enumerator around the corner. Since I had a checklist of which houses were standing in 1905 from the tax rolls and building permits, I could check further in the rolls for missing items. If the house was owner-occupied, I often had the name of the person I was looking for in the census since the tax rolls gave the owner's name in most cases. (I discovered whether the house was owner occupied by looking up the name on the tax rolls in the city directories.) I also checked the last few pages of every census district schedule with special care because persons not at home when the enumerator first made his rounds often appeared at the end.

The reliability of this method hinges on whether or not I missed families on the sample blocks who appear in the census schedules. (A certain proportion of families on the sample blocks were missed by the enumerator, but that it is not a defect of the method used here.) The total percent of dwellings standing in 1905 for which I could find no occupant, in the census, either because they did not appear there, or because my search method was inadequate, was 4.2 percent. This figure is sufficiently small that it can be attributed in the main to two factors: vacancies in housing units and omissions from the census. It is doubtful that this method would have yielded such complete results if I did not have a checklist of all houses standing in 1905 plus a partial list of the occupants. Others considering the use of this census schedule or any schedules, whether or not they contain house numbers, should spend the necessary time with the tax rolls to prepare a list of dwellings standing at the time of the enumeration. This is not a tremendously time-consuming operation since tax rolls are often arranged by street number or, as in Milwaukee, by subdivision, block, and lot number.

Sam Warner in his appendix to *Streetcar Suburbs* discusses some of the problems relating to the use of the census and its reliability. Warner adopted a rule of thumb of anticipating an error of ±6 percent in his population data. By indicating a possible error of 4.2 per cent I am not suggesting a reduction in Warner's estimate because certain households may still have escaped my research. Boarders were listed with the families with whom they lived, but boarders listed separately, or out of place in the schedules could have escaped my search, although I came across no cases of boarders listed separately. A more likely census error would be additional households living in a dwelling and listed out of place on the enumeration. Since many building permits indicated whether a dwelling was one-or two-family, it was possible to know whether to search further for a second household for a dwelling, but some building permits only listed structures as "residence."

APPENDIX B.

EVOLUTION OF PUBLIC SCHOOLS IN STUDY AREAS TO 1910[1]

LOCATION	DATE	DESCRIPTION
Ward 20 (established 1895)		
Teutonia and Hopkins	1873	opened, temporary quarters
	1877	closed
12th and Center	1877	opened, 2-room frame building
	1885	4 rooms added
	1898	new building opened, old frame building continued in use
22nd and Center	1887	opened
	1897	5 temporary classrooms in use
	1900	8-room addition opened, 3 temporary classrooms still used
15th and Hopkins	1894	opened
24th and Auer	1903	opened, 14 rooms
Ward 22 (established 1901)		
27th and Garfield	1893	opened
	1900	3 temporary classrooms in use
31st and Brown	1896	opened
	1900	3 temporary classrooms in use, another needed
28th and Clarke	1902	opened, 14 rooms
North and Lisbon	1905	existing school acquired by annexation
Ward 14 (established 1885)		
S. 15th and Forest Home	1875	opened, located on border between Wards 11 and 14
	1885	6 rooms added
	1891	ceased serving Ward 14
Becher and Windlake	1891	opened
	1900	2 temporary classrooms in use
	1902	100 students on half-day sessions
S. 10th and Hayes	1907	opened, 14 rooms
Ward 18 (established 1887)		
Cass, near Brady	1874	opened, just below ward boundary but continued to serve southwest corner of Ward 18
Prospect and Maryland	1879	opened
	1887	new building opened
	1900	3 temporary classrooms in use
Linwood and Bartlett	1901	2 temporary classrooms in use at location
	1902	12-room school opened

---

1 Milw. Board of School Commissioners, 1874-1910.

APPENDIX C.
CENSUS TRACTS INCLUDED
IN STUDY AREAS, 1940-1990

All census tracts were renumbered for the 1970 census; however, there were no changes in the boundaries of the tracts listed below.

1940-1960 NUMBER:	1970-1990 NUMBER:
Ward 14 Area:	
124	167
125	168
131	174
132	175
133	176
138	186
139	187
140	188
Ward 20-22 Area:	
39	62
47	63
48	64
49	65
50	66
51	84
52	85
64	86
65	87
66	88
67	89
68	90
69	98
77	99
78	100
Ward 18 Area:	
8	73
9	74
10	75
11	76
12	77
13	78
14	108
15	112

BIBLIOGRAPHY

I. PRIMARY SOURCES

1. Manuscript Sources

State Historical Society of Wisconsin, Madison.

Milw. Dept. of Public Works, City Engineer. MS. Maps Showing City and Ward Boundaries, 1848-1958.
Milw. Electric Railway and Light Co. 1909. MS. Map of T.M.E.R. & L. System in Milw. and Vicinity.
U.S. Bureau of the Census. 1879. MS. Schedules of the Manufacturing Census, Milw. Co., Wis.
----- 1880. MS. Schedules of the Tenth Census of Population, City of Milw., Wis.
Vliet, Garrett. 1835. MS. Plat of the Town of Milwaukee.
Wis. Secretary of State. 1905. MS. Census Rolls, Wards 14, 18, 20, 22, City of Milw.

Municipal Building, Milw.

Milw. Common Council. MS. Papers, 1880-1905. City Archives.
Milw. Dept. of the Building Inspector. Applications for Building Permits.
Milw. Dept. of City Development. 1994: Map and Inventory of Scattered Site Housing, Typescript
Milw. Dept. of Public Works, City Engineer. MS. Annexation Map of Milw.
----- Card File Showing History of Street Improvements in Milw.
Milw. Dept. of Public Works, Office of Sewer Engineer. MS. Atlases of the Sewer System of Milw.
Milw. Dept. of Public Works, Office of Water Engineer. MS. Atlases of the Water System of Milw.
Milw. Tax Office. MS. Tax Rolls of the City of Milw., 1888-1905. City Archives.

2. Published Sources

BAIST, G. W. 1898. *Baist's Property Atlas of the City of Milwaukee and Vicinity* (Philadelphia).
BEGGS, JOHN I. 1898. *Map of Electric Railway System: T.M.E.R. & L. Co.* (Milw.).
CASPAR, C. N. Co. 1904. *Caspar's Guide and Map of the City of Milwaukee* (6th ed., rev., Milw.).

----- 1907. *Official Quarter-Section Atlas of the City of Milwaukee* (Milw.).

----- 1914. *Official Quarter-Section Atlas of the City of Milwaukee Supplement* (Milw.).

CASPAR AND ZAHN. 1886. *The City of Milwaukee: Guide to the "Cream City" for Visitors and Citizens* (Milw.).

CHAPMAN, SILAS. 1891. *Map of the City of Milwaukee* (Milw.).

----- 1894. *Map of the City of Milwaukee* (Milw.).

MATTHEWS-NORTHRUP. 1891. *Map of Milwaukee, Wis.* (Buffalo and New York).

MILW. 1861. *Charter of the City of Milwaukee* Wm. Prentiss, Compiler (Milw.).

----- 1888. *General Ordinances with Amendments* (Milw.).

----- 1890. *Ordinances Regulating the Construction, Repairs, and Removal of Buildings in the City of Milwaukee* (Milw.).

MILW. BOARD OF PUBLIC LAND COMMISSIONERS, City Planning Division. 1946. *Population Changes by Census Tracts, 1920-1940* (Milw.)

MILW. BOARD OF PUBLIC WORKS. 1881-1911. *Annual Reports, 1880-1910* (Milw).

MILW. BOARD OF WATER COMMISSIONERS. 1873. *Communication and Report to the Common Council* (Milw.).

MILW. BOARD OF SCHOOL COMMISSIONERS. 1873-1910. *Reports, 1873-1910* (Milw.).

MILW. CITY COMPTROLLER. 1906. *Report, 1905* (Milw.).

MILW. COMMISSIONER OF PUBLIC HEALTH [George C. Ruhland]. 1916. *Housing Conditions in Milwaukee* (Milw.).

MILW. COMMON COUNCIL, SELECT COMMITTEE IN RELATION TO WATER WORKS. n.d. [Copy in the State Hist. Soc. of Wis. has the hand-written notation "1860-6l."] *Report* (n.p.).

MILW. DEPT. OF THE BUILDING INSPECTOR. 1964. *Annual Report* (Milw.).

MILW. DEPT. OF CITY DEVELOPMENT. 1962. *Milwaukee's Land Use Report* (Milw.).

------. 1992. *1990 Milwaukee Urban Atlas* (Milw.).

MILW. DEPT. OF HEALTH. 1891, 1892, 1901, 1906, 1909, 1911. *Annual Reports, 1891, 1892, 1901, 1906, 1908, 1910* (Milw.).

MILW. HOUSING COMMISSION. 1933. *Report of the Mayor's Housing Commission* (Milw.).

MILW. MAYOR'S STUDY COMMITTEE ON SOCIAL PROBLEMS IN THE INNER CORE AREA OF THE CITY: FACT FINDING COMMITTEE; SUB-COMMITTEE ON HOUSING CONDITIONS AND AVAILABILITY. 1960. *Report* (Milw.).

MILW. PARK COMMISSIONERS. 1906, 1909. *Annual Reports* (Milw.).

MILW. REDEVELOPMENT COORDINATING COMMITTEE. 1948. *Report: Blight Elimination and Urban Redevelopment in Milwaukee* (Milw.).

MILW. TAX COMMISSIONER. 1910. *First Annual Report* (Milw.).

MILW. CHAMBER OF COMMERCE. 1875. *Report for 1874* (Milw.).

----- 1888. *Report for 1887* (Milw.).

MILW. COUNTY, COUNTY CLERK. 1881-1917. *Statement Showing the Latest Statistics of Population and Matters Relating to the Assessment of Real and Personal Property, 1881-1917* (Milw.).

Milwaukee Sentinel. 1880-1910.

SANBORN MAP CO. 1910-1928. *Insurance Maps of Milwaukee, Wis. and Vicinity* (8 v., New York).

SANBORN AND PERRIS MAP CO. 1894. *Insurance Maps of Milwaukee, Wis.* (4 v., New York).

THOMPSON, CARL D. 1910. "The Housing Awakening II: Socialists and Slums--Milwaukee." *The Survey* 25: 367-76.

U.S. DEPT. OF STATE. 1843. *Sixth Census of Population, 1840* (Washington).

----- 1853. *Seventh Census of Population: 1850* (Washington).

U.S. DEPT. OF INTERIOR. 1864. *Eighth Census of Population: 1860* (Washington).

U.S. BUREAU OF THE CENSUS. 1883. *Tenth Census:1880, Statistics of Population* (Washington).

----- 1887. *Tenth Census: 1880, Report on the Statistics of Cities*, 19 (2 parts, Washington).

----- 1895. *Eleventh Census: 1890, Population* (Washington).

----- 1902. *Twelfth Census: 1900, Population* (2 v., Washington).

----- 1904. *Estimates of Population of Cities, 1901, 1902, 1903* (Washington).

----- 1905. *Special Reports: Street and Electric Railways, 1902* (Washington).

----- 1906. *Twelfth Census: 1900, Special Reports, Supplementary Analysis and Derivation Tables* (Washington).

----- 1912. *Thirteenth Census: 1910, Population* 1, 2 (Washington).

----- 1912a. *Thirteenth Census: 1910, Manufactures*, 8, 9 (Washington).

----- 1912b. *Thirteenth Census: 1910, Occupational Statistics* 4 (Washington).

----- 1912c. *Mortality Statistics: 1910*, Bull. no. 109 (Washington).

-----1912d. *Thirteenth Census: 1910, Supplements, Statistics for Wisconsin* (Washington).

----- 1913. *Thirteenth Census: 1910, Abstract of the Census* (Washington).

----- 1913a. *General Statistics of Cities, 1909* (Washington).

----- 1922. *Fourteenth Census: 1920, Population, Characteristics of Population by States*, 3 (Washington).

----- 1932. *Fifteenth Census: 1930, Population, Reports by States*, 3 (Washington).

-----1942. *Sixteenth Census: 1940, Population, Number of Inhabitants*, 1 (Washington).

----- 1942a. *Sixteenth Census: 1940, Population and Housing Statistics for Census Tracts, Milwaukee, Wis.* (Washington).

-----1952. *Census of Population and Housing: 1950, Census Tract Statistics, Milwaukee, Wis. and Adjacent, Area*, Bull. P-D 32 (Washington).

----- 1952a. *Census of Population: 1950, II Characteristics of the Population*, Part 13, Illinois; Part 22, Michigan; Part 32, New York; Part 35, Ohio; Part 49, Wisconsin (Washington).

----- 1962. *Census of Population and Housing: 1960, Census Tracts Final Report PHC(1)*, Part 21 Buffalo, N.Y. SMSA; Part 26, Chicago, Ill. SMSA; Part 28, Cleveland, Ohio SMSA; Part 40, Detroit, Mich. SMSA; Part 92, Milwaukee SMSA (Washington).

----- 1966. *Census of Manufactures, 1963, Area Statistics* 3 (Washington).

----- 1972. *1970 Census of Population and Housing: Census Tracts PHC (1)*, Report 35, Buffalo, N.Y. SMSA; Report 43, Chicago, Ill. SMSA; Report 45, Cleveland, Ohio SMSA; Report 58, Detroit, Mich. SMSA; Report 131, Milwaukee, Wis. SMSA (Washington).

----- 1983. *1980 Census of Population and Housing: Census Tracts, PHC80-2*, Report 106,Buffalo, N.Y. SMSA; Report 119, Chicago, Ill. SMSA; Report 123, Cleveland, Ohio SMSA; Report 140, Detroit, Mich. SMSA; Report 243, Milwaukee, Wis. SMSA (Washington).

----- 1993. *1990 Census of Population and Housing: Population and Housing Characteristics for Census Tracts and Block Numbering Areas, 1990 CPH-3*, Report 110-A, Buffalo, NY PMSA; Report 113B, Chicago, Ill. PMSA; Report 134B, Detroit MI PMSA; Report 231A, Milwaukee, WI PMSA.

U.S. CONGRESS, SENATE. 1911. *Cost of Living in American Towns*, 62nd. Cong., 1st Sess., Doc. no. 22 (Washington).

----- 1911a. *Reports of the Immigration Commission: Immigrants in Cities*, 61st Cong., 2nd Sess., Doc. no. 338 (2 v., Washington).

U.S. DEPT. OF INTERIOR, GEOLOGICAL SURVEY. 1958. *Milwaukee Quadrangle, Wis.-Milw. Co.*, 7.5 Minute series, topographic (Washington).

----- 1958a. Greendale Quadrangle, Wis.-Milw. Co., 7.5 Minute series, topographic (Washington).

WIS. 1874. *An Act to Revise, Consolidate and Amend the Charter of the City of Milwaukee* (Milw.).

WIS. BUREAU OF LABOR, Census, and Industrial Statistics. 1896. *Seventh Biennial Report* (Madison, Wis.).

WIS. BUREAU OF LABOR AND INDUSTRIAL STATISTICS. 1906, 1912, 1914. *Biennial Reports* (Madison, Wis.).

WIS. SECRETARY OF STATE. 1906. *Tabular Statement of the Census Enumeration of 1905* (Madison, Wis.).

Wright's City Directory of Milwaukee. 1881-1911. (Milw.).

Wright's Map of Milwaukee. 1897. (Milw.).

Wright's Map of Milwaukee. 1911. (Milw.).

Wright's Street Guide Supplement of Wright's City Directory. 1930. (Milw.).

II. SECONDARY SOURCES

BARTON, JOSEF. 1975. *Peasants and Strangers: Italians, Rumanians, and*

Slovaks in an American City, 1890-1950 (Cambridge, Mass.).

BECKLEY, ROBERT M. 1978. "The Effects of Federal Programs on Housing and the Quality of Life: The Milwaukee Case." In: John P. Blair and Ronald S. Edari, eds. *Milwaukee's Economy: Market Forces, Community Problems and Federal Policies* (Chicago).

BERNARD, RICHARD M. 1990. "Milwaukee: The Death and Life of a Midwestern Metropolis." In: Richard M. Bernard, ed., *Snowbelt Cities: Metropolitan Politics in the Northeast and Midwest since World War II.* (Bloomington).

BLANK, DAVID. 1954. *The Volume of Residential Construction, 1889-1950*, National Bureau of Economic Research, Technical Paper no. 9. Studies in Capital Formation and Financing (New York).

BODNAR, JOHN. 1976. "Immigration and Modernization: The Case of Slavic Peasants in Industrial America." *Jour. Social History* 10: pp. 44-71.

BOWDEN, MARTYN J. 1971. "Downtown Through Time: Delimitation, Expansion, and Internal Growth." *Economic Geography* 47: pp. 121-135.

Built in Milwaukee: An Architectural View of the City. 1983. (Milwaukee).

BURGESS, ERNEST. 1924. "The Growth of the City: An Intro-duction to a Research Project." *Publ. Amer. Sociol. Soc.* 18: pp. 85-97.

BYINGTON, MARGARET. 1910. *Homestead: The Households of a Mill Town* (New York).

CANFIELD, JOSEPH M. 1972. *TM: The Milwaukee Electric Railway & Light Company*, Central Electric Railfans Association, Inc. Bull. no. 112 (Chicago).

CHUDACOFF, HOWARD P. 1972. *Mobile Americans: Residential and Social Mobility in Omaha, 1880-1920* (New York).

COCHRAN, THOMAS C. 1948. *The Pabst Brewing Company: The History of an American Business* (New York).

CONZEN, KATHLEEN NEILS. 1976. *Immigrant Milwaukee, 1836-1860: Accommodation and Community in a Frontier* City (Cambridge, Mass.).

DERBY, WILLIAM EDWARD. 1963. "A History of the Port of Milwaukee, 1835-1910" (Ph.D. Dissertation, Univ. of Wis.).

DOLLAR, CHARLES M., and RICHARD JENSEN. 1971. *Historians Guide to Statistics.* (New York).

DOUCET, MICHAEL and JOHN WEAVER. 1991. *Housing the North American City* (Montreal and Kingston).

DREISER, THEODORE. 1989 [originally published 1911]. *Jennie Gerhardt* (New York).

EBNER, MICHAEL. 1988. *Creating Chicago's North Shore: A Suburban History* (Chicago).

EDARI, RONALD. 1978. "The Structure of Racial Inequality in the Milwaukee Area." In: John P. Blair and Ronald S. Edari, eds. *Milwaukee's Economy: Market Forces, Community Problems and Federal Policies* (Chicago).

EDEL, MATTHEW, ELLIOTT D. SCLAR, and DANIEL LURIA. 1984. *Shaky Palaces: Homeownership and Social Mobility in Boston's Suburbanization* (New York).

FELLMAN, JEROME D. 1957. "Pre-Building Growth Patterns in Chicago." *Annals Assoc. Amer. Geographers* 47: pp. 59-82.

FLEISCHMANN, ARNOLD. 1988. "The Territorial Expansion of Milwaukee: Historical Lessons for Contemporary Urban Policy and Research." *Jour. of Urban History* 14: 147-177.

FREEMAN, LINTON C. 1965. *Elementary Applied Statistics* (New York).

FRIED, JOSEPH P. 1972. *Housing Crisis U.S.A.* (Baltimore).

GALFORD, JUSTIN B. 1957. "The Foreign Born and Urban Growth in the Great Lakes, 1850-1950: A Study of Chicago, Cleveland, Detroit, and Milwaukee" (Ph.D. Dissertation, New York Univ.).

GILLETTE, HOWARD, JR. 1990. "Rethinking American Urban History: New Directions for the Posturban Era." *Social Science History* 14: pp. 203-228.

GITELMAN, HOWARD M. 1974. *Workingmen of Waltham: Mobility in American Industrial Development, 1850-1890* (Baltimore).

GLABERE, MICHAEL. 1992. "Milwaukee: A Tale of Three Cities." In: Gregory Squires, ed., *From Redlining to Reinvestment: Community Response to Urban Disinvestment* (Philadelphia).

GLASCO, LAURENCE A. 1977. "The Life Cycles and Household Structure of American Ethnic Groups: Irish, Germans, and Native-born Whites in Buffalo, New York, 1855." In: Tamara K. Hareven, ed., *Family and Kin in Urban Communities, 1700-1930* (New York).

GLAZER, NATHAN. 1967. "Housing Policy and the Family." *Jour. Marriage and the Family* 29: pp. 140-163.

GOHEEN, PETER G. 1970. *Victorian Toronto: 1850-1900*. Univ. of Chicago Dept. of Geography, Research Paper no. 127 (Chicago).

GREENE, VICTOR R. 1968. *The Slavic Community on Strike: Immigrant Labor in Pennsylvania Anthracite* (Notre Dame, Ind.).

HEGEMANN, WERNER. 1916. *City Planning for Milwaukee: What it Means and Why It Must be Secured* (Milw.).

HIRSCH, ARNOLD. 1983. *Making the Second Ghetto: Race and Housing in Chicago, 1940-1960* (Cambridge).

HOUSE, PATRICIA. 1970. "Relocation of Families Displaced by Expressway Development." *Land Economics* 47: pp. 75-78.

HOYT, HOMER. 1933. *One Hundred Years of Land Values in Chicago* (Chicago).

----- 1939. *The Structure and Growth of Residential Neighborhoods in American Cities* (Washington).

----- 1966. *Where the Rich and the Poor People Live*, Urban Land Institute Technical Bulletin no. 55 (Washington).

KASARDA, JOHN D. 1993. "Cities as Places Where People Live and Work: Urban Change and Neighborhood Distress." In: Henry G. Cisneros, ed., *Interwoven Destinies* (New York).

KATZ, MICHAEL. 1972. "Occupational Classification in History." *Jour. Interdisciplin. History* 3: pp. 63-88.

KEATING, ANN D. 1988. *Building Chicago: Suburban Developers and The Creation of Divided Metropolis* (Columbus).

KENNEDY, CHARLES. 1962. "Commuter Services in the Boston Area, 1835-1860." *Business History Rev.* 26: pp. 153-170.

KIRK, ROGER E. 1990. *Statistics: An Introduction* 3rd ed. (Fort Worth).

KNIGHTS, PETER R. 1971. *The Plain People of Boston, 1830-1860: A Study in City Growth* (New York).

KORMAN, A. GERD. 1959. "A Social History of Industrial Growth and Immigrants: A Study with Particular Reference to Milwaukee, 1880-1920" (Ph.D. Dissertation, Univ. of Wis.).

----- 1967. *Industrialization, Immigrants and Americanizers* (Madison, Wis.).

LAMPARD, ERIC E. 1961. "American Historians and the Study of Urbanization." *Amer. Hist. Rev.* 67: pp. 49-61.

----- 1963. "Urbanization and Social Change: On Broadening the Scope and Relevance of Urban History." In: O. Handlin and J. Burchard, eds., *The Historian and the City* (Cambridge, Mass.).

----- 1973. "The Pursuit of Happiness in the City! Changing Opportunities and Options in America," The Prothero Lecture, *Trans. Royal Hist. Soc.*, 5th ser., 23: pp. 175-220.

LARSEN, LAURENCE MARCELLUS. 1908. *A Financial and Administrative History of Milwaukee*, Bull. Univ. of Wis., no. 242, Economics and Political Science, ser. 4. (Madison, Wis.).

LEAVITT, JUDITH WALZER. 1975. "Public Health in Milwaukee, 1867-1910" (Ph.D. Dissertation, Univ. of Chicago).

LUBOVE, Roy. 1962. *The Progressives and the Slums; Tenement House Reform in New York City: 1890-1917* (Pittsburgh).

----- 1967. "The Urbanization Process: An Approach to Historical Research." *Jour. Amer. Institute of Planners* 33: pp. 33-39.

----- 1969. *Twentieth Century Pittsburgh: Community, Business, and Environmental Change* (New York).

LURIA, DANIEL D. 1976. "Wealth, Capital, and Power: The Social Meaning of Home Ownership." *Jour. Interdisciplin. History* 7: pp. 261-282.

McCLELLAN and JUNKERSFIELD, INC. 1928. *Report on Trans-portation in the Milwaukee Metropolitan District to the Transportation Survey Committee* (2 v., n.p.).

McKELVEY, BLAKE. 1949. *Rochester: The Flower City, 1855-1890* (Cambridge, Mass.).

----- 1956. *Rochester: The Quest for Quality, 1890-1925* (Cambridge, Mass.).

----- 1966. *The Urbanization of America, 1860-1915* (New Brunswick, N.J.).

McSHANE, CLAY. 1974. *Technology and Reform: Street Railways and the Growth of Milwaukee, 1887-1900* (Madison, Wis.).

MARSH, MARGARET. 1990. *Suburban Lives* (New Brunswick, N.J.).

MASSEY, DOUGLAS S. and NANCY A. DENTON. 1993. *American Apartheid: Segregation and the Making of the Underclass* (Cambridge, Mass.).

MAYER, HAROLD M., and RICHARD C. WADE. 1969. *Chicago: Growth of a Metropolis* (Chicago).

MILLER, ZANE. 1968. *Boss Cox's Cincinnati: Urban Politics in the Progressive Era* (New York).

MILW. REAL ESTATE BOARD. 1892. *Milwaukee! 100 Photogravures* (Milw.).

MONCHOW, HELEN CARBIN. 1939. *Seventy Years of Real Estate Subdivision in the Region of Chicago*, Northwestern Univ. Studies in the Social Sciences no. 3 (Evanston).

MULLER, EDWARD K. 1987. "From Waterfront to Metropolitan Region: The Geographical Development of American Cities." In: Howard Gillette, Jr. and Zane L. Miller, eds., *American Urbanism: A Historiographical Review* (New York).

NOLEN, JOHN. 1915. "Land Subdivision and its Effect Upon Housing." In: *Housing Problems in America*, Proceedings of the Fourth National Conference on Housing (Minneapolis).

----- 1929. *City Planning* (2nd ed., New York).

NORMAN, JACK. 1989. "Congenial Milwaukee: A Segregated City." In: Gregory Squires, ed., *Unequal Partnerships: The Political Economy of Urban Redevelopment in Postwar America* (New Brunswick, N.J.).

O'CONNOR, CAROL A. 1983. *A Sort of Utopia: Scarsdale, 1891-1981* (Albany).

ORUM, ANTHONY M. 1995. *City-Building in America* (Boulder).

OTTENSMANN, JOHN R. 1975. *The Changing Spatial Structure of American Cities* (Lexington, Mass.).

PRED, ALLEN R. 1966. *The Spatial Dynamics of U.S. Urban Industrial Growth, 1800-1914: Interpretive and Theoretical Essays* (Cambridge, Mass.).

REISSER, CRAIG THOMAS. 1977. "Immigrants and House Form in Northeast Milwaukee, 1885-1916" (M.A. Thesis, Univ. of Wis.-Milw.).

REPS, JOHN W. 1965. *The Making of Urban America: A History of City Planning in the United States* (Princeton).

RODWIN, LLOYD. 1961. *Housing and Economic Progress: A Study of the Housing Experiences of Boston's Middle-Income Families* (Cambridge, Mass.).

ROSE, HAROLD. 1970. "The Development of an Urban Subsystem: the Case of the Negro Ghetto." *Annals Assoc. Amer. Geographers* 60: pp. 1-17.

ROSENZWEIG, ROY. 1983. *Eight Hours for What We Will: Workers and Leisure in an Industrial City, 1870-1920* (Cambridge).

ROSSI, PETER. 1955. *Why Families Move: A Study in the Social Psychology of Urban Residential Mobility* (Glencoe, Ill.).

SCHMANDT, HENRY J., JOHN C. GOLDBACH, and DONALD B. VOGEL. 1971. *Milwaukee: A Contemporary Urban Profile* (New York).

SCHNORE, LEO F. 1965. *The Urban Scene: Human Ecology and Demography* (New York).

----- 1965a. "On the Spatial Structure of Cities in the Two Americas." In: P. Hauser and L. F. Schnore, eds., *The Study of Urbanization* (New York).

SCHORR, ALVIN L. 1963. *Slums and Social Insecurity,*. U.S. Dept. of Health,

Education and Welfare, Social Security Admin., Div. of Research Statistics, Research Report no. 1 (Washington).

SIMON, ROGER D. 1971. "The Expansion of an Industrial City: Milwaukee, 1880-1910" (Ph.D. Dissertation, Univ. of Wis).

SJOBERG, GIDEON. 1960. *The Pre-industrial City: Past and Present* (New York).

STACH, PATRICIA BURGESS. 1988. "Deed Restrictions and Suburban Development in Columbus, Ohio, 1900-1970," *Jour. of Urban History* 15: pp. 42-68.

STEFANIAK, NORMAN J. 1962. "Industrial Location Within the Urban Area: A Case Study of the Locational Characteristics of 950 Manufacturing Plants in Milwaukee County," *Wis. Commerce Reports*, 6, 2.

STILL, BAYRD. 1948. *Milwaukee: History of a City* (Madison, Wis.)

----- 1974. *Urban America: A History with Documents* (Boston).

STILLGOE, JOHN R. 1983. *Metropolitan Corridor: Railroads and the American Scene* (New Haven).

------ 1988. *Borderland: Origins of the American Suburb, 1820-1939* (New Haven).

SUTHERLAND, JOHN F. 1973. "Housing the Poor in the City of Homes: Philadelphia at the Turn of the Century." In: Allen F. Davis and Mark H. Haller, eds., *The Peoples of Philadelphia: A History of Ethnic Groups and Lower-Class Life, 1790-1940* (Philadelphia).

TARR, JOEL and JOSEF W. KONVITZ. 1987. "Patterns in the Development of the Urban Infrastructure." In: Howard Gillette, Jr. and Zane L. Miller, eds., *American Urbanism: A Historiographical Review* (New York).

TAUEBER, KARL E., and ALMA R. TAUEBER. 1969. *Negroes in Cities: Residential Segregation and Neighborhood Change* (New York).

TAYLOR, GEORGE ROGERS. 1966. "The Beginnings of Mass Transportation in Urban America." *Smithsonian Jour. of History*, 2 parts, 1, 2: pp. 35-50; 1, 3: pp. 31-54.

TEAFORD, JON C. 1979. *City and Suburb: The Politician Fragmentation of Metropolitan America: 1850-1970* (Baltimore).

TEMKIN, BARRY. 1970. "Oats and Iron: Horse Drawn Transportation in Milwaukee, 1850-1890" (B.A. Thesis, Univ. of Wis.).

THERNSTROM, STEPHAN. 1964. *Poverty and Progress: Social Mobility in the Nineteenth Century City* (Cambridge, Mass.).

----- 1973. *The Other Bostonians: Poverty and Progress in the American Metropolis, 1880-1920* (Cambridge, Mass.).

THERNSTROM, STEPHAN, and RICHARD SENNETT, eds. 1969. *Nineteenth Century Cities: Essays in the New Urban History* (New Haven).

TIEN, H. YUAN. 1962. *Milwaukee Metropolitan Area Fact Book 1940, 1950, and 1960* (Madison, Wis.).

VANCE, JAMES E., JR. 1960. "Labor-Shed, Employment Field, and Dynamic Analysis in Urban Geography." *Economic Geography*, 36: pp. 189-220.

----- 1967. "Housing the Worker: Determinative and Contingent Ties in Nineteenth Century Birmingham." *Economic Geography* 43: 95-127.

----- 1971. "Land Assignment in the Precapitalist, Capitalist, and Post-Capitalist City." *Economic Geography*: 47 pp. 101-120.

----- 1976. "The American City: Workshop for a National Culture." In: John S. Adams, ed., *Contemporary Metropolitan America* (4 v., Cambridge, Mass.).

VON HOFFMAN, Alexander. 1994. *Local Attachments: The Making of an American Neighborhood, 1850 to 1920* (Baltimore).

WALSH, MARGARET. 1972. *The Manufacturing Frontier: Pioneer Industry in Antebellum Wisconsin, 1830-1860* (Madison, Wis.).

WARD, DAVID. 1971. *Cities and Immigrants: A Geography of Change in Nineteenth Century America* (New York).

WARNER, SAM BASS, JR. 1962. *Streetcar Suburbs: The Process of Growth in Boston, 1870-1900* (Cambridge. Mass.).

----- 1968. *The Private City: Philadelphia in Three Periods of its Growth* (Philadelphia).

----- 1968a. "If All the World Were Philadelphia: A Scaffolding for Urban History." *Amer. Hist. Rev.* 74: pp. 26-43.

----- 1972. *The Urban Wilderness: A History, of the American City* (New York).

WHITBECK, RAY HUGHES. 1921. *The Geography and Economic Development of Southeastern Wisconsin*, Wis. Geological and Natural History Survey Bulletin no. 58 (Madison, Wis.).

WILKERSON, ISABEL. 1991. "How Milwaukee Boomed But Left Its Blacks Behind," *The New York Times* (March 19, 1991, A1).

WINNICK, LOUIS. 1957. *American Housing and its Use: The Demand for Shelter Space* (New York).

WOODS, ROBERT A., and ALBERT KENNEDY. 1969. *The Zone of Emergence: Observations of the Lower Middle and Upper Working Class Communities of Boston, 1905-1914*, Sam Bass Warner, Jr., ed. (2nd ed., Cambridge, Mass.).

WRIGHT, GWENDOLYN. 1983. *Building the American Dream: A Social History of Housing in America* (Cambridge, Mass.).

ZUNZ, OLIVIER. 1982. *The Changing Face of Inequality: Urbanization, Industrial Development, and Immigrants in Detroit, 1880-1920* (Chicago).

Index

process, 2-4; in Wards 20-22: 63-
64; in Ward 14: 84-87; in Ward
18: 107, 109
Subdivision: and city-building
process, 23-24, 119; in Boston,
6-8 ; of Wards 20-22: 55, 58;
Ward 14: 77-78; Ward 18: 101,
103, 105-106; and house size,
107
Suburbs, industrial, 22
Suburbanization, motivations for, 6,
119-120; twentieth century, 130;
see also City-building
process

Tax rolls, as source, 10
Tenancy status, *see* Homeownership
Tenements, 25, 40
Tenth St., 88
Teutonia Ave., 55
Thernstrom, Stephan, 8, 12
Third St., 22
Thirty-Fourth St., 62
Transportation, *see* Streetcars
Twelfth St., 76
Twenty-Eighth St., 61
Twenty-Seventh St., 52, 53
Twenty-Third St., 53

University of Wisconsin at
Milwaukee, 141
United States-born household heads,
see Native-born,

Urban Renewal projects, 131-133

Wahl St., 99
Warner, Sam Bass, Jr., 2,3 and
city-building process, 6-9; on
location of the upper class, 47; on
housing allocation and
suburbanization, 73; on sampling,
146
Washington, D.C. 5
Washington Park, 105
Water mains: in city-building
process, 4; extensions in network,
25, 28, 30; in Wards 20-22: 60,
63-64; in Ward 14: 84-87; in
Ward 18: 107, 109; wards
compared, 120
Weaver, John, 2, 11
West Allis, 22, 48
Whitefish Bay, 105
Wisconsin Ave., 20, 117, 127
Wisconsin Supreme Court, 130
Windlake Ave., 79, 88
Woods, Robert, 122
Workforce, 16-18, 122; *see also*
Occupational groups

Zeidler, Frank, 131
Zoo, County, 105, 120
Zunz, Olivier, 2